AVERY

AVERY

The Case Against Steven Avery
and What *Making a Murderer* Gets Wrong

KEN KRATZ

WITH PETER WILKINSON

BenBella Books, Inc.
Dallas, TX

BenBella Books, Inc.
10440 N. Central Expressway
Suite #800
Dallas, TX 75231
www.benbellabooks.com
Send feedback to feedback@benbellabooks.com

Printed in the United States of America
10 9 8 7 6 5 4 3 2 1

Library of Congress Cataloging-in-Publication Data is available upon request.
978-1-944648-00-8 (print)
978-1-944648-01-5 (e-book)

Editing by Alexa Stevenson
Copyediting by Scott Calamar
Proofreading by Michael Fedison and Rachel Phares
Text design by Aaron Edmiston
Text composition by PerfecType, Nashville, TN
Front cover design by Faceout Studio, Kara Davison
Full cover design by Sarah Dombrowsky
Printed by Lake Book Manufacturing

Distributed by Perseus Distribution
www.perseusdistribution.com

To place orders through Perseus Distribution:
Tel: (800) 343-4499
Fax: (800) 351-5073
E-mail: orderentry@perseusbooks.com

**Special discounts for bulk sales (minimum of 25 copies) are available.
Please contact Aida Herrera at aida@benbellabooks.com.**

For my son, Andrew

CONTENTS

FOREWORD

by Nancy Grace

After the murder of my fiancé many years ago, I abandoned plans to become a professor of Shakespearean Literature and instead entered law school. I had one and only one goal in mind . . . to put the truly bad guys in jail so innocent people could live free of the fear and violence that had destroyed my life and the lives of so many others.

Prosecuting in inner-city Atlanta for a decade, I ended every *voir dire*, or jury selection, with one simple question to each individual juror, singling them out specifically, one by one: *Can you listen to the facts and evidence presented in this courtroom and render a verdict that will speak the truth?*

The truth . . . a verdict that speaks the truth.

Fast-forward to years later to CNN's HLN *Nancy Grace* show. I still remember first hearing about a missing person, a lovely young woman, a photographer, Teresa Halbach. Her car had been found on the Avery salvage lot, but it was still hoped that Teresa herself was out there somewhere, alive. Sorting through literally hundreds of stories a day, hers struck a chord within me, and that's all it took—her disappearance would be one of the two to three stories that made it into the show that night.

I still can't fully explain what it was about Teresa that resonated with me. Maybe it was the brown eyes that looked at me from the photo we dug up of her, maybe it was her family's plea for help— to this day I don't recall. But I do recall one thing distinctly . . . that Steven Avery came onto the show live that night, and when the cameras stopped rolling, I spoke through my lapel mike to the executive producer behind me in our New York control room and said, very simply, *"He's lying."*

It went exactly like this:

Grace: I want to go straight out to the man you mentioned, Steven Avery. He is joining us by phone.

Steven, I understand that Teresa came to your auto salvage lot to take photos for the auto trader, correct?

Avery: Yes, she did. She came down by me.

Grace: OK, and, Steven, it's my understanding that also you state that you saw her car leave?

Avery: Yes, I did.

Grace: About what time?

Avery: She was there between 2:00 and 2:30.

Grace: 2:30 in the afternoon. OK, Steven, how is it that her car could get all the way back in this pit area where there is—well, I believe we're showing it right now. I mean, wouldn't she have to pass back by the office again?

Avery: Well, on the outskirts of the office, otherwise back by me, or back by (INAUDIBLE) pit in the corner, is all open.

Grace: It's all open?

Avery: Yes. Anybody can drive in there.

Grace: OK. So that says to me, Chuck Quirmbach, with Wisconsin public radio, that the assailant who took this girl would have to find her some distance away and then amazingly, incredibly, coincidentally take her car all the way back to Avery's auto salvage and park it back here in the pit with all these trashed cars.

Quirmbach: Well, we do have to say alleged assailant. We do not know the whereabouts of Ms. Halbach. We do not know if someone took her against her will to where the car was found.

(CROSS TALK)

Grace: OK. Chuck, Chuck, Chuck, a woman's point of view. I'm not going to park my car in a pit of junk cars and then go on vacation, OK? You might find my car at the airport, if I had a car, or maybe at the bus station or the train station.

So back to Mr. Avery. Mr. Avery, did you see anyone else come in, anyone unusual that didn't belong there?

Avery: Well, Thursday night, me and my brother had to go to Menards to pick up some wood with the flat bed. And I see taillights back by me. It wasn't supposed to be.

Grace: Yes.

Avery: But we turned around. And we went back there. The truck he parked on the side. And I took the flashlight on the flat bed, and I looked around by me and behind me, but I didn't see nothing.

Grace: Well, I want to point out, everybody, that Steven Avery is cooperating with police. He is not an official police suspect, and he is with us tonight speaking freely.

(COMMERCIAL BREAK)

(BEGIN VIDEO CLIP)

Unidentified Male: At 1:00 this afternoon, myself and my staff members met just to answer any other questions they may have had about the investigation. They remain hopeful.

(END VIDEO CLIP)

Grace: Teresa Halbach is missing. If you have any information, dial the sheriff's office (GIVES NUMBER).

Very quickly to Chuck Quirmbach. Are they sending in divers to search in the ponds in the area of the auto salvage?

Quirmbach: Yes. Apparently, that's been done. There's also apparently a large number of people checking fields around the Avery property. There's up to 200 people had been there investigating over the course of the last couple of days, so it's quite a wide net.

Grace: Mr. Avery, do you feel like you're being framed in any way?

Avery: Yes.

Grace: Why?

Avery: Because every time I turn around, the county's out here doing something to me.

Grace: In this case, do you think you're being framed?

Avery: Yes. I'm being set up, because of my lawsuit and everything else.

Grace: Because of your previous incarceration, you're suing?

Avery: Yes. They set me up then. And then . . .

Grace: Well, do you think it has anything to do with her car being found at your auto shop?

Avery: No. I tell you, it's because of my name and what they—what I went through from them.

Grace: But to Dr. Robi Ludwig, psychologist, of course, with her car—take a look at this—her car turning up in the middle of that, that is a very suspicious location.

Ludwig: Sure. But we do know that there are people that are wrongly convicted and that they do appear to be guilty and very often have to defend themselves once they're let out, and even if they are exonerated. So Mr. Avery is in a very difficult position.

Grace: And to Mr. Avery, is the pit back there where her car was found locked or fenced in? Can anybody just drive back there and leave their car?

Avery: Well, most of the time, no.

Grace: You mean it's normally not locked?

Avery: No. You can just drive right in and—if you wanted to drop something off, you could, you know?

Grace: OK, everyone, we'll keep you updated on the search for Teresa Halbach. Please help us bring Teresa home.

A big thank-you to all of my guests tonight. But our biggest thank-you, to you for being with us, inviting us into your homes.

I knew in my core that he was lying . . . but why? His story didn't add up. He told me, on national television, that Teresa Halbach had come to his auto salvage lot to take photos of a particular car, that she left and he never saw her again.

But what he told others on the day of Teresa's visit was quite the opposite. He told multiple people that Teresa "never showed up," and later, on the day she was reported missing, he repeated this tale to Teresa's roommate—and even called *Auto Trader* to complain about it. Then his story changed.

Why the subterfuge? Why lie to me about it on national television? Something that might have been explained away innocently, her visit to his auto lot, took on a much more sinister cast because of Avery's lies about it.

The evidence unfolded from there. Teresa's foreboding about her job assignment to Avery's place—she didn't want to go and said so. Her car found hidden at the far edge of Avery's property, hidden under plywood and other materials with Avery's skin cell DNA . . . *his skin cells on the hood latch of Teresa's car.*

Not only were the studs from the back pockets of Teresa's Daisy Fuentes jeans found, but her teeth and bones, burned beyond recognition, all found on Avery's lot in a "fire pit" tended all through the night by Avery himself, according to his own friends and acquaintances. This chilling scene divulged *not by police, but by Avery's own friends and relatives.*

Teresa's blood DNA was then found *on a bullet fragment discovered inside Avery's garage, fired from a gun found in Avery's own bedroom.* The physical evidence proving Avery murdered Teresa Halbach is overwhelming! And a jury that heard every shred of this evidence agreed.

Then . . . there is Brendan Dassey. I have reviewed Dassey's police interrogation tapes very carefully. He admits he assaulted Teresa and was there when she was murdered as well. Now the defense argues Dassey was too young to give a statement alone and is mentally impaired. In fact, Dassey's IQ falls within a normal range, and his mom knew he was speaking to police and chose not to sit in.

What matters here is only one thing, the same thing I reminded my jurors of all those years ago as a prosecutor. *The truth.*

This is not a popularity contest. Speaking the truth is more important than being named Miss Congeniality. No one, not me, and certainly not the prosecutor, is seeking that crown. It's a good thing, as our voices have been nearly drowned out by the media bandwagon, after a highly popular program pieced together ten from literally thousands of hours of footage and swayed thousands of viewers.

I am swayed by neither media hype nor television producers.

I am swayed by a search for the truth, regardless of what others may say. I am swayed by those deep brown eyes looking out from an old photo . . . looking at me, the jury, the media and everyone else who hears this case.

And I am swayed by the facts. By the overwhelming evidence that Teresa Halbach was lured to Steven Avery's auto salvage lot under the guise of a work assignment with her job at *Auto Trader*. The evidence that Avery murdered her and burned her body and tried his best to hide the evidence. That he is now caught in a tangle of lies and, but for a media outlet's highly produced "documentary," he would be forever branded as what he truly is . . . a murderer.

Prosecutors didn't "make him a murderer." He did that all on his own. The evidence says so.

And that, I submit, is the truth.

CHAPTER ONE

True Crime Today

My name is Ken Kratz. You may know me as the chief villain in the Netflix docuseries *Making a Murderer*, the ten-part television sensation released in December 2015 that ignited a fierce conversation in this country and beyond about whether or not our criminal justice system is rigged. The show became an international obsession, earned six Emmy nominations, and inspired too many internet sleuths and conspiracy theorists to count. It raised allegations of police and prosecutorial misconduct, suggested that evidence was tampered with, and left millions of viewers with the impression that a junkyard dealer named Steven Avery and his nephew, Brendan Dassey, were framed for the savage murder of a young photographer named Teresa Halbach.

As I watched the series, I wondered what had so riveted the public consciousness. It didn't feature dramatic reenactments, like

Errol Morris' *The Thin Blue Line* had, in 1988. No real-time car chases on California freeways, à la O. J. in 1994. No top-line actors portraying real people, as in *The People v. O. J. Simpson,* last year's O. J. redux. No reinvestigation by forensic professionals, like those recently featured on CBS "solving" the twenty-year-old murder of child beauty queen JonBenét Ramsey.

Timing and technology, I thought, underpinned *Making a Murderer*'s success. The show burst out during an electric, transformative, pre-Trump period in our country. Notoriously conservative America seemed to be leaning left, newly willing to challenge law enforcement. Many of the police shootings that fueled the Black Lives Matter movement resulted in no charges being filed against cops (think Baltimore, Ferguson), and yet the American public clamored for the freedom of a white man, Steven Avery, who was, by any measure of the evidence, stone guilty. This fascinated and, frankly, surprised me. When *Making a Murderer* took home four Emmys, it seemed that those who judge popular culture had sanctioned a newfound activist spirit, if one inconsistently applied.

Obsession with a convoluted case and the accused's guilt or innocence is nothing new. Some of us may remember Cleveland neurosurgeon Sam Sheppard who, in 1954, was convicted of killing his pregnant wife, Marilyn. Speculation, often about facts not in evidence, ran rampant, both in the newspapers and on "new media"—at the time, television. Sheppard won a new trial as a result, and walked free.

Making a Murderer also benefited from a thundering shift in the media climate, from the advent of "hot take" internet journalism to fact-parched online forums and social media. Thanks to the internet, a piece of bad information can be repeated so many times in so many places so quickly that it becomes accepted as true, and the uniquely vitriolic atmosphere of internet comment sections inspires people to say things they never would in person.

The series birthed its own virtual family, whose members—by turns supportive and loyal, vengeful and vindictive, incurious and glib, each spinning varying theories of the truth—kept the argument about Steven Avery's role in the death of Teresa Halbach boiling twenty-four hours a day, every day. In that way, *Making a Murderer* represented, perfectly, true crime as it's understood now.

True crime, with real-world consequences.

Making a Murderer so influenced public opinion about Avery's guilt that more than 500,000 Americans signed a petition demanding executive clemency for this unrepentant killer—even though the president has no authority to grant such a pardon for state charges. As lead prosecutor for both the Avery and Dassey trials, I was painted as responsible for a blatant miscarriage of justice in the most notorious murder case in Wisconsin since the trial of serial killer Jeffrey Dahmer in 1992.

I've been ridiculed relentlessly across the blogosphere—my heavyset appearance jeered at, and my high, thin voice mocked. On talk shows and in newspapers I've been called corrupt, incompetent, and narcissistic. At my law office in Superior, Wisconsin, thousands of death threats and abusive messages poured in via email and telephone. Men wrote that they wanted to rape and kill my daughter while I was forced to watch. Fortunately, I don't have a daughter.

To escape the vitriol, I shut down my Twitter feed and restricted my Facebook account. I closed my law office in April 2016 after hundreds of negative internet reviews posted by complete strangers drove my practice into the dirt.

For years since Avery's 2007 conviction, out of respect for the family of Teresa Halbach—the actual, and often overlooked, victim in this case—I tried to remain above the fray. Unlike the defense team, I did not participate in *Making a Murderer*, declining an interview request made in February of 2013. I appear in the series only in opportunistically edited archival TV footage, at press conferences and in court.

If you've watched *Making a Murderer*, you know about the deplorable things I did in the years following Avery's conviction: sexting a domestic abuse victim, and making inappropriate advances toward other women. If you judge me harshly, I don't blame you. Rest assured, my punishments fit my crimes. I lost everything: my wife, my career, my house, my life savings, and my reputation. After inpatient rehab for sex addiction, I've been "clean" for more than six years. Yet even today, I'm defined by my regrettable past.

This book isn't intended to polish my tarnished image, vent my anger, or ask for sympathy. I am writing it because the truth matters, and people get hurt when it is twisted and misrepresented. More public horror has been expressed at the imagined plight of Steven Avery than at Teresa's very real murder. We live in a time when the police have lost our unquestioning trust, and the American justice system is no longer assumed to reflect the ideal of fairness upon which it was founded. But if we begin with the assumption that *no one* can be trusted, our criminal justice system can't function.

So why should you believe a word I have to say?

That's easy. I'm not asking you to.

The bulk of my argument centers on the physical, scientific evidence against Avery: the blood, the key, and the burn pit. I'm going to present the damning evidence and testimony that was omitted from the Netflix series. And I'm going to demonstrate that it would require a conspiracy of absurd proportions to cook up the sheer volume of evidence pointing toward Avery's guilt, and to keep its creation secret.

Making a Murderer is filled with distortions and omissions— editorial choices that slanted the show to the defense perspective at almost every turn. I will highlight the most obvious omissions for you and expose what really happened between 2005 and 2007. I will walk you through the case point by point, and when I'm done, I think you'll agree that Steven Avery earned his cell in the Waupun Correctional Institution, where he'll sit until he dies.

Avery became a killer on October 31st, 2005, the day he stole the life of an innocent twenty-five-year-old. I didn't make anyone a murderer. I did my job, and convicted one.

CHAPTER TWO

The Disappearance

As Calumet County district attorney, my office in Chilton, Wisconsin, bore little resemblance to the opulent book-lined chambers grandly occupied by Adam Schiff and Jack McCoy in *Law & Order*, but it was mine and I liked it. I'd hung a few paintings by my dad, a professional wildlife artist, mostly of ducks and geese. He worked for the Milwaukee Public Museum, creating special exhibits and painting the backgrounds of their dioramas—the kind of stuff you see in any visit to natural history museums (dinosaurs, buffalo being taken down by Native American hunters, and settlers taming the prairie).

Outside my window, on the first floor of a three-story brick building on Court Street, I saw a cheese factory (still operating!) and fertile farm fields (miles of them)—it would be hard to find two more stereotypical symbols of the state of

Wisconsin. *Making a Murderer* did an estimable job of portraying our corner of the state as forlorn and Wisconsinites as judgmental and unfriendly, but in truth small-town Wisconsin is distinguished by a sense of family, and of belonging to a community that enjoys uncomplicated pleasures. The Green Bay Packers football team, who play their home games thirty minutes northeast of our county line, is owned not by some mendacious billionaire hell-bent on hoodwinking credulous locals into buying new stadiums with taxpayer dollars, but by the community itself. Residents can purchase a share or two in the team, meaning Cheeseheads, including me, aren't just spectators: we have ownership equity! Fairs and festivals and tailgate parties—where people laugh at bad jokes as smoke curls up from sausage-laden charcoal grills, where you can hear "Roll Out the Barrel" echoing through the crowd and watch strangers dancing the polka with each other—that is Wisconsin life, and I make no apologies for it. It is the life I love, even now, after all that's happened.

By 2005, I had been the county's elected district attorney for thirteen years. A couple of high-profile cases came my way—including prosecuting a local couple who'd forced their seven-year-old daughter to spend nights in a dog cage—but only a few homicides, none of which went to trial. Like other medium-sized DAs' offices in Wisconsin, we made do with just one other attorney and a tiny support staff.

On November 3rd, 2005, Mark Wiegert, one of four full-time Calumet County sheriff's investigators, knocked on my door.

"You're not going to believe this," Mark said, as he sat down in a chair opposite my desk, sporting his usual small goatee and rural Wisconsin uniform—an earth-toned sweater, khaki pants, and comfortable shoes.

A young woman named Teresa Halbach had been reported missing that morning. She hadn't been heard from since Halloween—Monday, October 31st, a day she'd spent freelancing for *Auto Trader* magazine, taking pictures of vehicles people wanted to sell.

"Guess where Teresa was last seen?"

Not in the mood for games, I waved at Mark to continue.

"At Steven Avery's salvage yard."

On dusty and rutted Avery Road, in rural Mishicot, in the northern half of Manitowoc County, to be precise.

"THE Steven Avery?"

"Yup," Mark said, leaning back with a *how-do-you-like-them-apples* expression on his face.

Wisconsin mints few celebrities. But Steven Avery enjoyed star status; a few even considered him a local hero. Avery had been convicted in 1985 for the sexual assault and attempted murder of a prominent Manitowoc County businesswoman, Penny Beernsten, winning his freedom in 2003 after crime lab DNA expert Sherry Culhane, at the behest of the Wisconsin Innocence Project, matched a pubic hair from the original case file to a convicted sex offender named Gregory Allen.

I'd served with Penny a couple of years before on the Wisconsin Crime Victims Rights Board, a five-person panel appointed to review alleged violations of victims' rights by judges, DAs, cops, and other criminal justice professionals—at the time the only sanctioning body of its kind in the country. Penny had a tough time navigating the exoneration process, and had been guilt-ridden over having misidentified her attacker in 1985, both in a photo array and live police lineup, at a time when Steven, twenty-three, had five children, including twin sons only a few days old.

Like everyone in the area, I'd heard about Avery's $36 million lawsuit against Manitowoc County in the wake of his exoneration. He was all over the news, supported by Innocence Project lawyers, a sitting governor, and Wisconsin legislators who'd even named a new criminal justice reform law after him, and I knew his name attached to a missing person case would mean extra scrutiny for everyone—including me.

───────────────

Citizen search efforts began that Thursday, headed by Teresa's younger brother, Mike, her roommate, Scott Bloedorn, and his friend (and Teresa's former boyfriend) Ryan Hillegas. After guessing the password to Teresa's online cell phone records, Teresa's friends phoned numbers Teresa had called on Monday, and pieced together a schedule of her appointments. When Bloedorn called Steven Avery on Thursday, November 3rd to ask about *his* appointment with Teresa, Avery said she'd never shown up.

Missing person flyers soon blanketed Manitowoc County storefronts, public buildings, lampposts, and even the Avery salvage yard business office. In this close-knit area that I've been describing, Teresa had accomplished the impossible: she'd vanished without a trace. Many Wisconsinites, including me, suspected foul play, and the perpetrator, we thought, must be an outsider, some big-city transient, some junkie or tweaker or pill head from Milwaukee or Chicago passing through—not one of our own.

Years later, Avery's defense lawyers, Dean Strang and Jerry Buting, would make much of Teresa not being reported missing between Monday, October 31st and Thursday, November 3rd, a period of three days. Perhaps, suggested Steve's erstwhile New Dream Team—now darlings of social justice zealots worldwide— Teresa had run off and did not want to be found. Maybe she intended to go missing. Or, as Jerry Buting had the temerity to suggest, maybe some secret, sordid lifestyle choice had caught up with her.

But a twenty-five-year-old woman does not live under the microscope of parents and friends. Teresa's roommate, Scott, worked construction and their hours often did not overlap. She operated her freelance photography business out of shared space in Green Bay and sometimes, if a job ran late, slept over with friends there.

That Wednesday, November 2nd, Teresa didn't show up at her Green Bay studio, as she usually did after a standing weekly appointment. When she still hadn't checked in the next morning (Thursday, November 3rd), Tom Pearce, Teresa's colleague and mentor, called her mom, Karen Halbach. Now Karen was worried.

Compounding matters, Teresa, a volunteer coach, missed practice for her little sister's middle school volleyball team. Coach Teresa showed up on time to every practice and every game, without fail. Usually, she hustled in half an hour early, to check uniforms and gear, her Powershot A310 camera slung over her left shoulder, ready to chronicle small triumphs of her eager players.

Was Teresa alive, or dead?

I feared I knew the answer to that question, and so too did Mark Wiegert. Reliable, kindhearted Wisconsin girls don't just disappear without a word to family or friends. Teresa hadn't walked off the face of the earth; someone had snatched her from it. Before closing this case, we would encounter a strain of evil, a pitiless vortex of vindictiveness, that none of us had experienced before.

Two days into the investigation, on Saturday, November 5th, we caught our first break: Teresa Halbach's SUV turned up. Where? On the Avery salvage lot, hastily covered with tree branches, plywood, and an old car hood. A search plane we'd sent up on Friday had failed to spot it. Ironically, the RAV4 was detected in the most low-tech way possible—by a volunteer citizen searcher, operating on foot.

That searcher happened to be a second cousin of Teresa's, a local private investigator named Pam Sturm. In *Making a Murderer*, it's made to appear that Sturm was sent to the Avery property by the team coordinating the search. We see the defense lawyers questioning one of the search leaders about why he gave

Pam, and only Pam, a digital camera. In fact, Pam asked to borrow the camera. She also specifically asked to search the Avery property. She knew it was the last place Teresa had been seen, and it seemed only logical to search the salvage yard full of cars to see if Teresa's might be one of them.

Odd as it may have seemed, Pam, faced with forty-plus acres and over 3,800 cars to search, simply got lucky out of the gate by beginning her search in the southeast corner of the sprawling Avery junkyard (near the business parking area). Nothing more. Nothing less. Nothing conspiratorial. Nothing nefarious about it. Also, consider this: if Pam, as the Avery defense team later suggested, was somehow complicit in framing Steven Avery in the disappearance of Teresa Halbach, why would she "find" her cousin's car so suddenly and under circumstances that could be interpreted as, if not sketchy, then beyond the realm of pure happenstance? Also, the RAV4's license plates had been removed. They would be found two days later, crumpled and hidden inside another junked vehicle on the salvage lot.

When I arrived that Saturday afternoon, parts of Highway 147, the main route to the Avery property, had already been closed off by police. I drove down Avery Road, past the salvage business buildings, and met my Calumet County cops, including Sheriff Jerry Pagel and Investigator Mark Wiegert, in the business parking area. Together with representatives of the Manitowoc Sheriff's Department and DA's Office, we agreed that, given the pending Avery civil lawsuit, in order to avoid any appearance of impropriety, Manitowoc County sheriff's officers would play only a supporting role in the Halbach investigation.

As the Manitowoc DA believed his office had the same potential conflict, I accepted appointment as special prosecutor. As good a detective as Mark Wiegert was, I knew we needed additional investigative expertise, and we needed it fast. This was a big case, and Calumet law enforcement still had a whole county to serve. Sheriff Pagel put in a call to the Wisconsin Department of Justice's Department of Criminal Investigation (DCI), the state body tasked with investigating crimes deemed "statewide in nature or importance." Nobody could argue that this case didn't fit squarely under that bland rubric.

That same Saturday, Tom Fassbender had planned to spend the afternoon at his home in Appleton, parked in front of the TV with his wife, Kathy, watching the Wisconsin Badgers play football. The Division of Criminal Investigation homicide specialist was a tall (6'4"), laconic fellow of mostly German stock, who'd faced off in cinder-block, sweat-stinky investigation rooms with his share of killers, and put most of them behind bars, often getting them to talk themselves into their very own prison-orange wardrobe. Fastidious, with an unyielding sense of purpose, he'd trained a fair share of the law enforcement recruits and evidence techs in the state. Tom enjoyed a reputation around Wisconsin as a homicide detective who went by the book, never "tuned-up" suspects, as is portrayed on every cop procedural show on television, and was impossible to corrupt. Leaving Kathy and the

Badgers behind, driving his state-issued Ford Taurus, he clocked the ninety-minute drive to Mishicot in about an hour.

Eyeing an expanse of twisted, rusting metal, hulks of automobiles and trucks brought there by age, death, or destruction, Fassbender wondered if he'd ever find the clues he needed. Those metal skeletons, surrounding quarry pits, and the elements might, Tom knew, conceal them forever. Or maybe there were no clues; maybe, just maybe, Teresa was still alive.

As there were nowhere near enough "non–Manitowoc County" evidence techs on the scene, it was decided that the three most experienced Manitowoc Sheriff's Department officers on location, Lieutenant James Lenk (head of the detective unit), Detective Dave Remiker, and Sergeant Andrew Colborn (head of the patrol division), would have to assist with the search. Fassbender determined that the three had virtually no connection to the 1985 Avery assault case, but instructed that, as members of the Manitowoc Sheriff's Department, officers Lenk, Remiker, and Colborn would not be allowed to search any area of the salvage property on their own; they'd be accompanied by a search team leader—either a Calumet County evidence tech or a DCI special agent.

"A search for Teresa, or evidence as to where she might be, had to get completed that first night," Fassbender recalls. "We didn't have the luxury of calling upon hundreds of trained search personnel, as larger jurisdictions might, so we ensured the search teams consisted of experienced law enforcement officers who had little or no connection to Steven Avery." After obtaining our first search warrant for the property, those teams set off, shortly before 4 PM that Saturday afternoon, hoping to find signs of Teresa.

A major storm was rolling in, and an enclosed trailer was on the way to transport Teresa's SUV to the crime lab in Madison, where it could be processed away from the elements. Tom ordered an officer to place a tarp over the SUV, in case rain hit before the trailer arrived. He wanted to prevent any evidence present on the outside of the vehicle, such as fingerprints or DNA, from being washed away. And so the tarp was secured over the RAV4 . . . until the winds picked up. Now fearing the shifting tarp might itself disturb the branches and other debris atop the car, Fassbender had the tarp removed. Of course it was then, as Murphy's Law dictates, that it began to rain—sheets of the stuff. Despite Tom's unflinching decisiveness, things had gone to shit quickly.

Meanwhile, sniffer dogs set to work, including Brutus, a well-behaved Belgian Shepherd, part of the Great Lakes Search and Rescue K-9 group. Brutus was a cadaver dog, trained to detect the scent of human remains, more particularly, decomposition—blood, bone, and tissue. When alive, each person in the world has their own unique odor, and "live-scent" search dogs are typically given an article of the missing person's clothing to smell. Cadaver dogs, in contrast, do not need clothing or anything else to complete their task, because they specialize in the smell we all share after death—the unmistakable aroma of decay. After scuffling to and fro, Brutus alerted on Teresa's RAV4.

In that moment, our missing person case became a likely homicide—and everyone at the scene knew it.

———————————

As evening fell, live-scent and cadaver dogs zigzagged in and out of the sea of junked cars, hitting on dried bloodstains inside many of the vehicles, the result of crashes that had deposited them in this hopeless dump in the first place. But as the search-and-rescue canine teams approached the Avery trailer, another dog, Bear, Steven Avery's vicious German Shepherd, growled and paced, preventing any searcher, two- or four-legged, from getting anywhere near the burn pit located directly behind Avery's garage. With all the other areas to be searched that night, it didn't seem like a big deal. Anyway, any junkyard dog protects its turf.

Three days later, that burn pit is where we'd discover Teresa Halbach's charred remains.

CHAPTER THREE

The Victim

In *Making a Murderer*, viewers enjoyed a sweet glimpse of Steven Avery; they saw baby pictures and snapshots of him as a gap-toothed kid, heard about how much he loved his wife, and how overjoyed he was by the birth of his twin boys. We didn't hear much about Teresa Halbach, the woman he murdered. That's fine: the series wasn't about Teresa. But this book is, in part, dedicated to her memory, and in this chapter, before I tell you what we know about Teresa's last day and how she came to cross paths with Steven Avery, I want to show you who she was, and what was lost when she was killed. Before delving into analysis of blood and bone fragments, I want to remind you that this was the blood and bone of a charming, funny young woman—an avid traveler, a long-distance runner, a farm girl turned summa cum laude graduate, a sister and a friend.

Photographing cars for sale—tough to find a more mind-numbing endeavor. But Teresa was soon getting out of that. The photo shoot at the Avery salvage yard on October 31st, 2005, was the last she planned to do for *Auto Trader* magazine. Her Monday side job with them had become more of a hassle than it was worth—too much travel, too little money, too many leering scumbags like Steven Avery.

Meanwhile, her portrait business in Green Bay had expanded, in part because Teresa had a knack for photographing children—difficult subjects many photographers strenuously avoid. "Teresa loved babies," recalls her friend Kim Peterson. "Teresa would say, 'You know how parents say *this job must be birth control for you*? Well, it's just the opposite for me.'" Patient and serene, Teresa could also be silly. As a result, children adored her.

To my mind, some of the most heart-wrenching images surrounding the entire case come from a candlelight vigil held in Sherwood, Wisconsin, Teresa's hometown, on Monday, November 7th, after the RAV4 had been discovered, but before the gruesome contents of the burn pit were recovered. There was still hope that Teresa would be found alive. Players from the middle school volleyball team that she coached lit candles and sang songs alongside Teresa's family, friends, and complete strangers who'd turned up to show support for the Halbach family.

Teresa was especially close to her sisters. At Avery's trial, Teresa's sister Katie pressed back tears as she recalled Teresa returning from a shopping trip not long before she died. She'd purchased a pair of Daisy Fuentes Jeans, named for the MTV

Star and Revlon spokesmodel. Katie had teased her about them, calling them "old person jeans." It had become a running joke between the sisters. Investigators found a rivet from a pair of Daisy Fuentes jeans in the burn pit behind Steven Avery's garage—a discovery not mentioned in *Making a Murderer*. Katie Halbach also identified a blue National Guard lanyard, which Teresa had attached to her car key. The lanyard was recovered hidden from view inside the center console of the RAV4. At the end of the lanyard was a black plastic clip, designed to connect to a matching blue key fob—the fob discovered on November 8th, the day after the vigil, in Steven Avery's bedroom, the key to Teresa's vehicle still attached. The lanyard and key fob had been a gift from Katie to her sister.

Since her breakup with Ryan Hillegas, her high school sweetheart, Teresa had not been in a serious relationship. Teresa Halbach's friend Trinity Rosenow rejected the notion that Teresa went home one night with the wrong person. "She rarely dated," Rosenow says. "When Jerry Buting blamed her lifestyle for her murder in his closing argument, I almost jumped up and smacked him. He didn't know how important her Catholic faith was to her. How dare he."

But Teresa, it seemed, had caught the eye of one local man— divorced, with five children, a criminal record, and a girlfriend who drank too much—Steven Avery, of Avery Road, Mishicot. When he called *Auto Trader* at 8:12 AM on October 31st to make his Halloween-day appointment, Avery asked them to send "the photographer who had been out there before." He wanted Teresa.

Auto Trader is a throwback. In it, owners of used vehicles advertise them for sale—not online, not on Craigslist, or CarSoup.com—but in the pages of an actual, printed magazine. Imagine that! In a state steeped in tradition, *Auto Trader* remained the first and best option for Cheeseheads who wanted to rid themselves of their used cars and trucks. Thousands of vehicles changed hands via *Auto Trader* every year. It might have taken more time than e-commerce, but it still achieved solid results—a Wisconsin article of faith.

That day, Avery took steps to conceal himself. Unwilling to give his name or phone number to *Auto Trader* when booking the shoot, he provided "B. Janda" as a contact name and a telephone number belonging to his sister, Barb Janda. He'd recently convinced Barb to list her red 1989 Plymouth Voyager for sale, despite the fact that she wasn't much interested in selling it. He promised to pay the forty-dollar fee, set up the photo shoot, and take care of the whole process himself.

While on the road, Teresa left a message on Barb Janda's voice mail, a tape of which was played at the beginning of Episode 2 of *Making a Murderer*, "Turning the Tables." Well, most of it: five seconds of the call disappeared—the part where Teresa says she's not sure where she's going.

Message Played in *Making a Murderer*	Uncut Message
"Hello, this is Teresa with *Auto Trader* magazine. I'm the photographer, and just giving you a call to let you know that I could come out there today, um, in the afternoon. It would probably be around two o'clock, or even a little later. Um, again, it's Teresa. If you could please give me a call back and let me know if that'll work for you. Thank you."	"Hello, this is Teresa with *Auto Trader* magazine. I'm the photographer, and just giving you a call to let you know that I could come out there today, um, in the afternoon. It would—will probably be around two o'clock, or even a little later. But, um, if you could please give me a call back and let me know if that'll work for you, **because I don't have your address or anything, so I can't stop by without getting the—a call back from you**. And my cell phone is [XXX-XXXX]. Again, it's Teresa, [XXX-XXX-XXXX]. Thank you."

Teresa had taken pictures for Steven Avery and his family before. In fact, she'd been out to the Avery place on five previous occasions. That fifth time, after phoning Teresa directly to set up the appointment on a forty-six-degree October 10th, Steven Avery answered his door clad in only a small white towel. Creepy, thought Teresa. She told friends and coworkers she didn't want to return.

The fact that Teresa had been to the Avery property several times before was an important argument for the defense, and for their claim that "Teresa knew exactly where she was going and who she was meeting with" on the afternoon of October 31st. And it's true that by that afternoon, when Teresa spoke to *Auto Trader*'s receptionist Dawn Pliszka again, she had figured out that she was on her way to the salvage property of "The Avery Brothers."

But Teresa had photographed cars for other members of the family at the Avery salvage property, including Tom Janda, Barb's estranged husband. If Steven wanted Teresa to know where she was going and the man she'd be meeting, why not use his own name, instead of "B. Janda"? Why not call Teresa directly on her cell phone to book the appointment as was done just three weeks before on October 10th—he had the number—unless, as I strongly suspect, he realized that after the towel incident she'd be unwilling to return?

Here's something else *Making a Murderer* didn't mention: Steve did call Teresa that day, twice early in the afternoon before Teresa's arrival, blocking his number using *67. And it's not like he blocked his cell number habitually—he did not use *67 for *any* of the more than one dozen other calls he made that day. The audience of *Making a Murderer* may not have heard this evidence, but the jury did, and they understood its significance. They heard the *full* unedited voice mail message, left at Barb Janda's number, with Teresa saying she didn't know where she was headed, along with the evidence about Steve's call blocking—they understood that

Steven Avery was attempting to keep Teresa from knowing where she was going, and more importantly, who she'd be meeting with on her arrival. The man who'd enjoyed and even courted the spotlight in Wisconsin for so long after his spectacular exoneration— who couldn't stay out of the public eye, condemning cops and lawyers with relish, changing laws and shaking hands with politicians, judges, and reporters—now, for some reason, wanted to be a ghost. A spooky ghost at that.

———————

Teresa was off and on her phone all day before she arrived at the salvage yard. She screened calls, but if a message was left for her, she called back right away. Teresa regularly checked her voice mail messages, was "almost obsessive about it," according to those who knew her well. But after her visit with Avery on the afternoon of October 31st, 2005, her phone was never used again. Cell records show that 2:41 PM that day was the last time it was in service.

That same afternoon, witnesses smelled burning plastic and saw fire coming from the burn barrel in front of Avery's house. Teresa's phone, camera, and PDA were recovered from that same burn barrel—Steven Avery's burn barrel—on Sunday, November 6th. *Making a Murderer* never mentioned the recovery of Teresa's burned electronics.

Teresa may not have used her phone after her arrival at Avery Salvage, but Steven Avery called her one last time that day, late that afternoon, at 4:35 PM—two hours after, records show, her phone was already turned off and likely disabled. This time, however, he didn't bother with *67. Why? Maybe because he knew she was already dead—perhaps because he was standing over a burn barrel, calling the phone as it melted in the flames, to be sure it had been successfully destroyed.

Whatever the reason, he knew Teresa wasn't going to answer. He would float the story that Teresa never showed up for the photo shoot and stick with that story until around 5 PM on Thursday, November 3rd—this call was Steven Avery's first attempt at misdirection.

CHAPTER FOUR

The Perpetrator

Yes, in 1985, Steven Avery was convicted of a sexual assault and attempted murder that he did not commit. At some point, the Manitowoc Sheriff's Department either knew, or should have known, that they had the wrong man. They could have, and should have, worked harder to secure his release after uncovering compelling evidence of his innocence. Avery was entitled to compensation. He got it—$400,000, what he settled for in his lawsuit against the county.

That doesn't mean Avery was a Boy Scout. Far from it. Mr. Avery had been a busy, committed criminal—and pervert—since his teen years spent wandering among skeletons of condemned metal. That is to say, Avery's status as a suspect in the 1985 assault shocked few in law enforcement—he had a long rap sheet by then and a history of violence, especially against women. The redoubtable Steven was a suspect in a Marinette County sexual assault that occurred around Memorial Day 1985, not even sixty days before the Penny Beernsten assault. Local police and sheriff's squad cars were a common sight on Avery Road, long before Teresa Halbach lost her life.

The first we hear of Avery's history in *Making a Murderer* is from Avery himself:

> *"I really ain't got much on my record. Two burglaries with my friends. We just rode around, get something to do. And we decided to rob a tavern and that . . . was the first time I got busted with them friends. Crawled into the bar through the broken window to steal fourteen dollars in quarters and two six-packs of Pabst beer and two cheese sandwiches."*

Hey! That's not so bad! He was probably hungry! What Steve and *Making a Murderer* don't tell you is that it wasn't a simple matter of crawling in through a broken window to get beer and sandwiches. In fact, Avery ripped a board off the tavern window, went inside, and vandalized the business, breaking things, smashing bottles, and spreading charcoal around on the floor and on the pool table, causing hundreds of dollars of damage. He'd been convicted of another burglary as a minor, but those records are sealed.

Next up in *Making a Murderer* is an unfortunate incident with a cat in 1982:

> *"Another mistake I did . . . I had a bunch of friends over, and we were fooling around with the cat . . . and I don't know, they were kind of negging it on and . . . I tossed him over the fire . . .*

and he lit up. You know, it was the family cat. I was young and
stupid and hanging around with the wrong people."

Actually, on that September day, Avery suggested burning a
cat alive. He and his buddies built a bonfire. Steven doused the
cat in gas and oil before the stricken animal was thrown onto
the fire. It jumped off and ran around the yard, still ablaze, until
Avery caught the cat, applied additional fuel, and threw it back
on. No "mistake," or "hanging around with the wrong people"—
this was intentional, sadistic animal cruelty.

Perhaps the most shocking—and shockingly edited—episode
in Avery's criminal history is his encounter with his second cousin,
Sandra Morris, in the winter of 1985. In *Making a Murderer*, we
hear that Sandra was picking on "Stevie."

Then:

"Steve, can you tell me in your own words why you ran Sandy
off the road and pointed a gun at her?"

"Because she was spreading rumors that I was on the
front lawn and on the road, bare ass, and she was telling
everybody about it, and it wasn't true."

The incident itself is described via a recorded interview
between Avery and a law enforcement officer.

"I seen her come by and then I went down the road and I just
pulled alongside of her. And then we hit and she went into a
little skid."

"Was your gun loaded?"
"No, it was empty. The shells were at home."

Here's the complete story, not available on Netflix. Avery had been in the habit of standing on the road outside his property early in the morning and exposing himself to Sandra Morris when she drove by on her way to work. Morris didn't report the incidents, a neighbor did, and when police contacted Morris to confirm and file the official report, she was reluctant to get him in trouble because, she said, he was "family." She mentioned to the officer that she'd told Steve's father about the problem and was hopeful it might stop on its own, without involving law enforcement.

At 5:30 AM on the day in question, as Sandy Morris drove along Old Highway Y, a car rushed up behind her. The vehicle pulled alongside as if to pass and then rammed into the side of her car, forcing it off the road. Sandy jumped out of her car, as did the other driver—an angry Steven Avery, brandishing a rifle.

He pointed the gun at Sandy and ordered her to get in his car. She begged Steven not to shoot her, and told him she wasn't alone. She had her one-year-old daughter in the car, to be dropped off with Sandy's parents on the way to work. "She'll freeze to death," Sandy said. She asked him to let her go and drop off her daughter, promising that afterwards she would come back and he could do whatever he wanted.

Keeping the gun pointed at his cousin, Avery peered inside. After verifying that her baby was indeed in the vehicle, he let Sandy go, but followed her down the road for a while before turning around and roaring back toward home. When Morris got to her parents' place, she called 911.

When police arrived at Avery's, they asked about the rifle. Steven had hidden it—under the bed of one of his sleeping children. Cops found a live round in the icy rifle's chamber. The gun, of course, was not empty after all.

Steven Avery pled guilty to felony reckless endangerment, and a judge sentenced him to six years in prison—years that would end up being served concurrently with his sexual assault sentence. When you hear about the eighteen years he served for a crime he didn't commit, please remember that six of those eighteen years were served for a crime he did.

Avery's history of domestic violence against his young wife, Lori, is also well documented, going back to the early '80s. He choked, hit, and punched her. He once found her in a battered women's shelter and had to be forcibly removed. Lori firmly believes that if Steven hadn't been sent to prison in 1985, he'd have killed her.

If you've seen *Making a Murderer*, you know that after Steven's 1985 incarceration in the Penny Beernsten case, Lori received hate-filled and threatening letters from him, including promises to kill and mutilate Lori upon his release—and drawings of how he would do it. Lori, Steven felt, wasn't bringing their five children to see him in prison often enough, and had said she wanted a divorce.

You also heard Steven claim that Lori "took the kids away from me." The real story, however, is that circuit court judge Fred Hazelwood ordered Steven Avery to have no contact with his children, even while he was incarcerated. Why? Because some of the letters he'd sent were *addressed directly to his kids*, and contained missives like "I hate mom; she will pay," "I will get you when I'm out," and "Daddy will git mom when daddy gits out."

Of Steven, Hazelwood said: "The kind of threats he made to his wife, not simply a threat to kill her, but this grandiose mutilation-type scheme, the drawings, and everything else indicate that this is not simply a thought of an instant, this is something that he has brooded over for some period of time and has not been able to deal with in any effective manner"; and, "He has huge anger. He has real potential to harm people." Even when the no-contact order was later lifted, only one of Steven's five children, a teenaged daughter, appeared at the prison to greet him upon his release.

Next up is Steven Avery and Jodi Stachowski: a Wisconsin love story. Their relationship was depicted in *Making a Murderer* as a tender one that only unraveled during the Halbach investigation. It was, you might think watching the series, yet another casualty of the corrupt criminal justice system. In fact, Stachowski suffered near-constant emotional and physical abuse at the hands of Steven Avery during their two years together.

In September of 2004, after a 911 call, officers made contact with a very frightened Jodi Stachowski. When they asked what had happened, Jodi, looking backward toward the truck where Steven was sitting, said "she couldn't tell [them] right now." Once

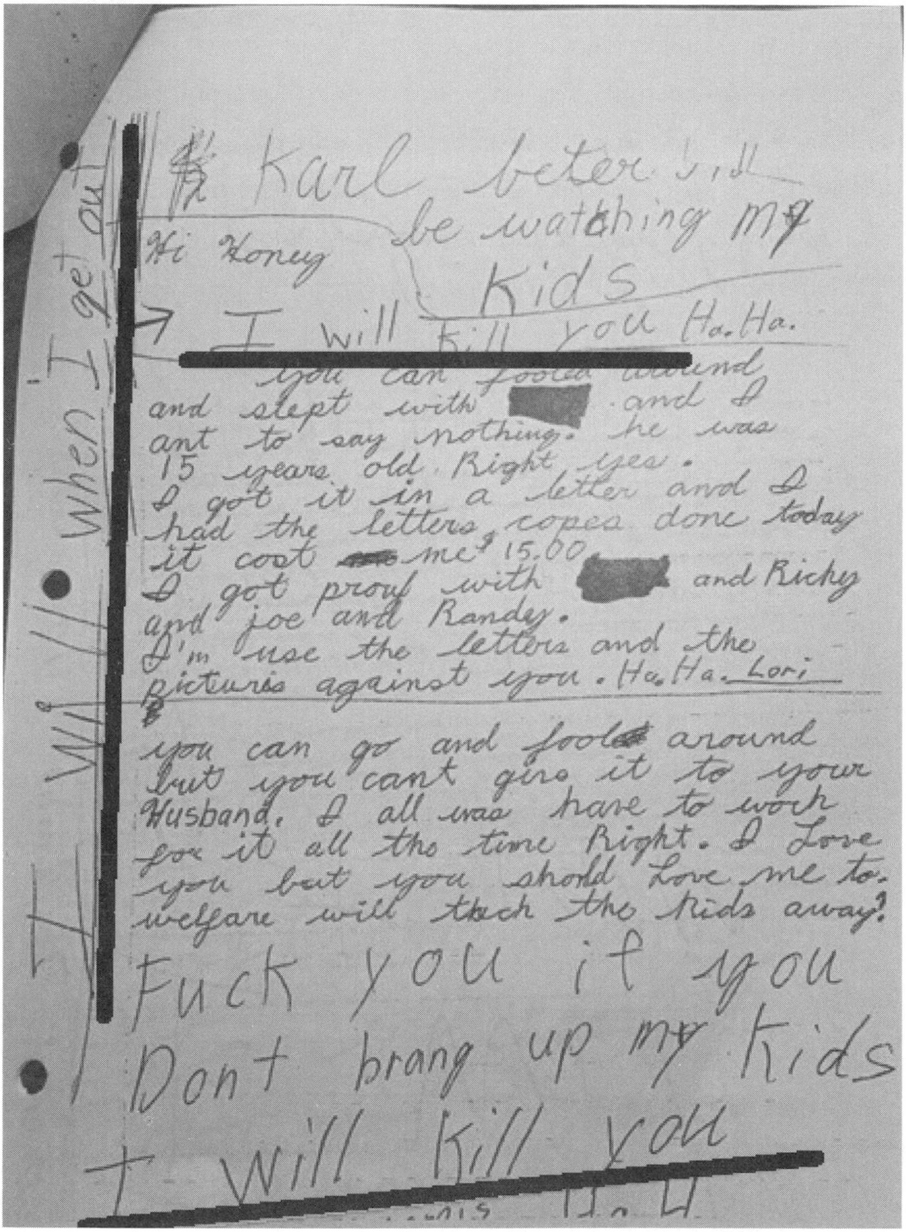

One of Steven's letters to Lori

she was farther away, she reported that Steven Avery had assaulted her in their trailer, hit, and strangled her. Avery himself confirmed the two had been fighting (over Jodi's whereabouts and failure to answer her phone), but insisted that he'd only pushed Jodi down. Ms. Stachowski declined to write a formal statement, and the deputies filed the matter under the heading "family fight," simply charging Steven with an ordinance violation of disorderly conduct, and allowing him to pay a small fine.

In interviews with officers during the time *Making a Murderer* was being filmed, in 2005 and 2006, Jodi detailed other incidents—once, Avery choked her until she blacked out, and when she came to she was on the floor, Avery trying to drag her out the front door of the trailer. In *Making a Murderer* we see a spliced-together clip of this very interview, but none of the footage is of Jodi discussing her abuse. Jodi's abuse by Steven was confirmed by neighbors and family. Avery often threatened to kill Jodi if she left him, just as he'd threatened his ex-wife, Lori, before and during their divorce in the 1980s.

————————————

Then there are the rape allegations. In 1982 or 1983, while living with his wife Lori, Steve is said to have attacked their nineteen-year-old babysitter, J. A. R., in his home, holding the victim's hands over her head and raping her. If she breathed a word of the assault to anyone, he promised, he would kill her and her family. This witness didn't tell her story until Avery had already been charged with murder, and naturally some people believe it is part of the multilayered "conspiracy" against Avery. Another incident, however, might be harder to dismiss.

In the summer of 2004, Steven Avery, forty-two, allegedly raped his seventeen-year-old niece, M. A., in his sister Barb's trailer. True to form, Avery threatened to kill the teenaged female relative, and her family, if she reported the assault. The rape was initially reported to authorities by the girl's mother; the girl herself only agreed to cooperate with prosecutors after Avery was safely locked up for the Halbach murder the following fall. Jodi Stachowski told law enforcement that Avery justified having intercourse with M. A. by saying they were not actually "blood relatives," as M. A. had been adopted by one of Steven Avery's siblings.

The rape case proceeded, to be prosecuted by John Zakowski of the Brown County DA's Office, but was put on hold pending the results of Avery's murder trial. After the murder conviction in 2007, the DA, in consultation with the victim, decided not to subject the girl to the additional ordeal of a rape trial, and closed the case.

By the time of his arrest in the Halbach case, law enforcement had chronicled years of abusive and even what experts would later identify as "typically sociopathic" behavior by the explosive Steven Avery. Animal abuse is often exhibited by those who later turn their violence toward humans. Rumors of inappropriate conduct between Avery family members themselves didn't surprise any of the cops or prosecutors. But rumors aside, what was known for certain was that although Steven Avery had turned out to be innocent of the Beernsten assault, he was still a dangerous and criminally savvy alum of the Wisconsin prison system. The

Steven Avery we had known for years bore little resemblance to the soft-spoken and polite character that would be introduced to the world in *Making a Murderer*.

From the bleak, clattering Manitowoc County Jail, both Steven Avery and Brendan Dassey made regular phone calls after their arrests, mostly to Avery family members, in which they discussed speculations, strategies, and often contradicted statements made earlier to law enforcement investigators. Steven used the phone to attempt to manipulate his family, directing them to talk to Brendan about not taking a plea agreement, complaining that they weren't trying hard enough to post his bond, or weren't following his directions regarding defense strategy. Like most prisoner calls to the outside world, they were collect calls, and expensive—what "Pa Avery" complained were nine dollars a minute.

Those calls provided a window into the two men's personalities, and *Making a Murderer* makes frequent use of them in its ten episodes, culling snippets and playing them back, accompanied by subtitles. The calls are a spectacular storytelling mechanism for the show, by turns chilling, pathetic, sorrowful, funny, and infuriating. Filmmakers Laura Ricciardi and Moira Demos came up with their unique jailhouse phone call approach after prison officials prevented them from visiting or filming Steven in prison. Ironically, the voice of Steven Avery was often captured on a jailhouse phone in the days before and just after Teresa Halbach disappeared, while he was a free man. His fiancée, Jodi Stachowski, was in the local lockup, serving a seven-month sentence for her fifth DUI conviction.

Many *Making a Murderer* viewers wondered if Avery knew his jailhouse calls were being recorded. Of course he knew. He's a seasoned convict, a guy who knows how jails operate. Before each and every call is connected, a mechanical voice warns the inmate and call recipient that they are being monitored and recorded. Standard operating procedure, on any tier, in any corrections facility nationwide.

In fact, Steven Avery used the jail calls to shore up his defenses and float theories for later use. He is acutely aware of being recorded as the news breaks that Teresa Halbach is missing. While speaking to Jodi on November 3rd, 2005, Steven tries to establish an alibi: "I called Teresa after she left on that day [October 31st]," he tells Jodi. "And I wondered why she didn't have her phone turned on."

Perhaps the most evidentially relevant are the calls between Jodi and Steven the day of the murder itself: October 31st, 2005. At 5:37 PM, after Teresa is either dead—lying lifeless in the rear cargo area of her Toyota RAV4—or still tied up at the Avery property, Jodi places her regular late-afternoon call from the local jail.

Sounds of Steven spitting are interrupted with groans and the occasional "Uh-huh," as if he is pretending to listen, but the multitasking killer is clearly on autopilot as he continues his conversation with Jodi. As I listened to the call, considering what had just occurred, or might still be occurring, I found its casual nature unsettling. Steven talks about his new "big TV" and having moved his Jeep and snowmobile out of the garage—a task that would have been required to back Teresa's SUV inside.

At about 9 PM, Jodi calls again. Steven, by that time, is pre-occupied. In the background, a police scanner chirps, undoubt-edly to warn Avery in case Teresa is reported missing and police begin a search for the photographer. His admission to Jodi that he "brought Brendan over here with me tonight" foreshadows the statement Brendan Dassey would make to law enforcement officers four months later—that he helped his uncle tidy up the crime scene, helped hide the victim's SUV on the salvage prop-erty, and helped dispose of the victim's body in the fire.

Most important is Avery's talk of the fire itself. *Making a Murderer* never mentions that in his early interviews with law enforcement, Steven Avery denies having had a fire the night of October 31st. Many witnesses will see the fire and testify at trial fifteen months later, but when officers first ask Avery what he did the night of Halloween, he says he was home alone in bed. In fact, Avery not only doesn't mention the fire, he denies even having a "burn pit," and then eventually allows that he has one, but that nothing had been burned in it for two weeks. Brendan doesn't mention the fire in his early interviews either, and Steven doesn't mention that Brendan was over that night at all.

Why not mention the fire, if there was nothing suspicious about it? What's more, if you were being interviewed as the last person known to have seen a missing woman, why would you give "home alone in bed" as your alibi if you had a teen nephew as an alibi witness? Surely it would have been easier to say, "I was home cleaning out the garage and having a bonfire—ask my nephew Brendan, he'll tell you." Granted, you might not want to mention a burn pit if you knew the bones of the twenty-five-year-old woman you'd killed were in there, waiting to be recovered by the cops.

What's also important, in my view, is what Steven does *not* tell Jodi during these calls on the day of Teresa Halbach's disappearance. Usually, no detail is too mundane to warrant a mention between Steven and Jodi, and yet Steven never once lets on that a photographer was there to take pictures of a van, or that he himself had secured her attendance that same morning. He certainly doesn't mention that he had taken off work that entire afternoon, for the first time ever, presumably to complete the brief transaction with Ms. Halbach.

In the days immediately following the murder, Steven talked about having used a Rug Doctor to shampoo all the carpets in his trailer, and Jodi suggests that he clean the inside of the rug shampoo machine, a task that Steven hadn't thought of until his talk with his fiancée; he then says he may even "take this Rug Doctor" back to a local home improvement store and trade it in for a new one. But not until the media announcement, on November 3rd, that she is missing, will Steven and Jodi discuss Teresa's visit three days prior. Any law enforcement investigator will tell you that "consciousness of guilt" can be shown through what a suspect says, but also what he does not say—mentions that arise only belatedly, when events would more typically be discussed on the day they occurred.

On October 30th, 2005, the day before Teresa's last, Avery, his voice angry and taut, speaks with Jodi several times. He is obsessing over whether Jodi has somehow betrayed him by getting a job without his permission. (She hasn't.) He's determined to control all aspects of his fiancée's life, even while she's locked up. He fixates on how much of his money Jodi spends, rages over the size of his phone bill, bloated by expensive jailhouse calls. He monitors Jodi's commissary purchases, her clothing allowance, and bitches about the number of cigarettes she smokes.

In a call early that Sunday evening, Jodi casually mentions showering that day, after lunch. Avery doesn't hear her say "after lunch"—he is sure Jodi said she showered "after work."

Not a big deal, right? On the contrary! Over the next several hours, in repeated phone calls between the two, Avery continues to browbeat Jodi, demanding to know where she works. Jodi has no job—she's locked up—and she explains that obvious fact over and over: that she's jobless and she simply showered "after lunch." Jodi having an income, not controlled by Steven, would be unacceptable, and so the shouting match goes on and on.

"You said 'after work'!" Avery seethes.

"I said after lunch!" Jodi replies.

"I heard you say 'after work'!"

"You heard me wrong. I said after lunch!"

"Where do you work?"

"Shut up!"

"Where do you work?"

Avery pummels his fiancée with questions about her nonexistent job more than ten times in the space of a couple of minutes.

The argument ends with Avery threatening not to accept calls from Jodi for a week. "If you want to keep pushing my fucking buttons and piss me off like that again, then you know what will happen," he warns.

I've listened to hundreds of hours of Avery phone calls, and reviewed written reports of hundreds more hours I didn't have time to hear personally. One thing has become crystal clear: Steven Avery cares about one person in this world—Steven Avery—and the rest of the world's population, immediate family included, are given Steve's time and attention only to the extent that they can help him.

After serving her seven months on the drunk driving charge, Jodi Stachowski leaves the Manitowoc County Jail in March of 2006. Steven is himself now in the Calumet County Jail awaiting trial on the Halbach murder charge, and Jodi is reluctant to continue living on the salvage compound with Avery's family. Calls between Jodi and Steve turn chilly, and even more contentious. Soon their relationship will dissolve.

Nearly ten years later, in January of 2016, Jodi Stachowski gave an interview for the *Nancy Grace* show on the HLN network describing the terror she lived with during her relationship with Steven Avery. According to Jodi, she approached the *Making a Murderer* filmmakers before the series aired, asking that her comments in their documentary be removed, because they were "all lies," the product of Avery's threats and manipulation. Steven said "she'd pay" if she did not participate in "the movie project" (eventually to become the Netflix series) and say "good and nice" things about him. Jodi invited anyone who didn't believe her to listen to the recorded jailhouse phone calls in which Avery threatened her and demanded her continued cooperation.

Like Steven's ex-wife Lori, Jodi feels lucky to have gotten out of her relationship with Avery alive.

"He's not innocent," she said in the interview—no longer willing to cover for her ex, who has been locked up long enough for her to recover a sense of safety. After his wrongful conviction, she explains, Avery believed "all bitches owed him."

Jodi believes that Teresa was just unlucky enough to have been standing there when Steven decided to collect on his debt.

CHAPTER FIVE

The Blood

Blood.

A centerpiece of countless murder cases, an evidentiary linchpin.

And so it was that blood, his own and that of his victim, landed Steven Avery in prison for life.

Blood can be a boring subject. The science surrounding it makes most people's eyes glaze over—including mine, sometimes, and juries can fall asleep during "blood" testimony by experts who work with blood every day, who analyze it, trying to determine what its presence means when people die at the hands of others.

But blood does not lie. Blood tells truths—incontrovertible truths of the same sort told by DNA testing. I'd be willing to take a blood oath to that effect.

If you want to truly understand the case against Steven Avery, and how and why his defense lawyers tried so desperately to manipulate the blood evidence, you must wrap your arms around the complexities of blood—spatter, EDTA, DNA, and so on. Please understand, as I take you through this bloody story, no pun intended, that blood—what it represents and the information we can glean from it—has come a long way since O. J. was riding down LA freeways in his white Ford Bronco.

So, here we go.

Fully visible smears and drops of blood were found in Teresa Halbach's RAV4, on the front passenger seat, the driver's seat, the floor near the center console, on a CD case, on the dashboard near the ignition, on a panel between the rear door and cargo area, and pooled on the inside wall of the cargo area itself. If you watched *Making a Murderer*, you probably came away regarding the blood evidence in a sinister, nefarious light, as proof of a conspiracy, proof that two dedicated Manitowoc sheriff's deputies with spotless records had sneaked into that SUV, and squeezed droplets of blood from a purple-topped vial stashed in their pockets.

Well, folks, the explanation for how that blood ended up in the RAV4 is far simpler. Some of it came from Teresa, when she was shoved into the cargo area of her own SUV, as Avery tried to figure out how to dispose of her body. And some of that blood dripped from a deep cut on the right middle finger of Teresa Halbach's killer, one Steven Alan Avery.

After Brutus alerted on the SUV, signaling to his handler that human remains—most likely blood—were present inside the locked car, the vehicle was transported to Madison for processing. Beginning November 6th, evidence techs in Madison at the Wisconsin State Crime Lab photographed bloodstains, collected samples, and ran preliminary tests. These first tests determined the blood was human, both male and female. The male blood obviously didn't belong to Teresa. Was it Avery's? Did the female blood belong to Teresa? Answers to these two questions, obviously, were central to the case. And after further testing, it would become indisputable that the answer to both questions was *yes*.

Teresa's blood was found in the rear cargo area—according to experts, the blood pattern showed that this was where her bloodied hair had rested against the side panel. Crime lab experts found Steven's blood in six places in the victim's car. For a minute, let's discuss "blood pattern" evidence—it was the *way* the blood was deposited in the SUV that enabled the experts (and ultimately the jury) to decide *how* the blood got there. This would become critical after the defense alleged that crooked cops planted Steven Avery's blood from a vial found in the clerk's office. Was the blood observed in the SUV consistent with this planting theory, or was the pattern of bloodstains more complicated, suggesting other specific human mechanisms?

Nick Stahlke, Wisconsin crime lab expert, testified that the different bloodstains attributable to Steven Avery had been left in different ways. Specifically, the stain on the driver's seat and stain located in the rear cargo area were both "passive" droplets. That's the dripping kind of blood deposit you might expect to find on your counter or your floor at home, as gravity causes the blood to fall to the surface. Nothing complicated there, and those two stains don't exclude the "planting" theory, but it was important to have shown them to the jury for comparison. For one thing, Steven Avery had a cut on his finger. This actively bleeding cut is where those droplets of blood came from.

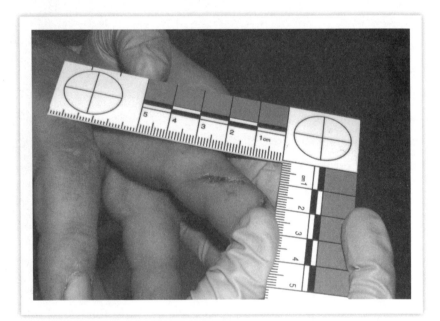

Cut on Steve's finger at time of arrest

Avery's blood recovered from a CD case came from a "contact transfer" stain, meaning that the part of Avery's body that was bleeding (his right middle finger) came into contact with the CD case and left the stain. There was also a contact transfer stain on the front passenger seat cushion. Perhaps the most recognizable bloodstain from the entire trial was the blood of Steven Avery "swiped" across the victim's dash, near her ignition, in a motion that was consistent with turning a car key. Stahlke was able to "show" the jury how Steven Avery's finger caused the stain pattern: the bloody finger makes contact with the ignition area, and leaves the swipe of blood as it moves across the surface.

Investigators found similar stains in similar driver's-seat locations in Steven's own car.

Think about all of this for a second. Would cops plant "droplets" of blood in one area of the RAV4, then plant contact transfer blood on the CD case, ignition area, and elsewhere? Why? Artistic whim? How could they guarantee that Steve would have a cut on his finger providing the source for the "actively bleeding" stains?

The DNA testing that determined that the blood belonged to Steven Avery was performed by crime lab unit chief Sherry Culhane. Coincidentally, she's the same analyst who tested the pubic hairs sent to the lab with fingernail scrapings in 2003, matching one to Gregory Allen and winning Avery his freedom. Questioned during the trial by Milwaukee County Assistant District Attorney Norm Gahn, who himself holds a master's degree in forensic science, Culhane explained her work in the Avery case. How ironclad was the evidence that the blood in question was Steven's?

> **Gahn**: Did you arrive at a statistical number for this profile that would reflect how often, or how rare, or how common, this profile would be in the population?

Culhane: Yes, I did.

Gahn: And could you explain to the jurors what that statistic is?

Culhane: This number tells me that the probability of another unrelated, random person in the population having the same profile as the evidence samples that we just talked about is one person in four quintillion in the Caucasian population.

Gahn: And does that statistic also apply to the other bloodstains that you found in the RAV4 that were attributable to Steven Avery?

Culhane: Yes, it does.

As you can imagine, especially in our post–O. J. world, this presented a major stumbling block for the defense. Arguing that the blood didn't belong to their client wasn't possible. Instead, they'd have to explain how it got in the victim's vehicle—they would argue it was planted.

On or before July 20th, 2006, the defense team learned that a box was present in the Manitowoc County Clerk of Circuit Courts Office, purportedly containing a vial of Steven Avery's blood. They used the existence of this vial to begin developing their "planting" defense, essentially the centerpiece of their representation of Steven Avery. That vial of blood had been drawn in 1996, during Avery's assault appeal, and after being used to develop Avery's DNA profile, it was returned to the clerk's office, where it sat for a decade, through the post-conviction motions and hearings that exonerated Avery of the 1985 sexual assault and attempted murder of Penny Beerntsen.

Avery's defense team asked the *Making a Murderer* filmmakers to film the vial's location and condition. Under no obligation to advise the state of the existence of this explosive potential evidence, Ricciardi and Demos waited for the defense attorneys to disclose the evidence, which they would not do for another five months.

If Ricciardi and Demos were asked by the defense attorneys to film the evidence in July 2006, and the attorneys were confident that the filmmakers would not share this major event with the prosecution, it seemed clear to me that these two film students— that's what they called themselves back then, though they were known around town and in local media as "the Avery PR team"— were not so much impartial chroniclers of the trial process as they were involved in the process themselves, as an investigative or technical resource for the defense.

When I discovered that they knew about the blood, had assisted with its documentation, and were even interviewing potential trial witnesses, I had to wonder: What else did they discover, and likely share, with the defense attorneys that the State was not provided? I wanted to see their video and have the same access to this information granted the defense.

I filed a motion in the circuit court for Manitowoc County, asking the judge to order Ricciardi and Demos to turn over all the video and audio of phone calls, relevant face-to-face interviews of witnesses, and the footage of their clerk of court's recordings from July 2006—all information highly relevant to the prosecution of Steven Avery. Through their attorney, Robert Dvorak (the same Robert Dvorak featured in Episode 10 of *Making a Murderer* as lead counsel for Brendan Dassey's post-conviction defense team), the filmmakers objected and asked that the judge quash the subpoena, claiming they had no evidence the State didn't already have, and that they had never shared any of their materials with the defense attorneys. Citing First Amendment law, a high hurdle that prosecutors in this position regularly fail to clear, the court agreed.

Well, I tried.

———————

But back to that blood vial. In Episode 4 of *Making a Murderer,* we see one of Avery's defense attorneys, Jerry Buting, arrive at the Clerk's office to examine the box containing the vial of blood—it only became "evidence" the day the defense team said they intended to use that blood as the "source" of blood in Teresa's SUV.

We see close shots of the broken seal on the box that contains the vial of blood. We do *not* hear that the seal was broken in the presence of Avery's own Innocence Project defense team in 2002, in a meeting to review the available physical evidence for retesting in pursuit of his eventual exoneration.

We hear Mr. Buting enthuse about a "tiny little hole, just about the size of a hypodermic needle," seen in the cap of the vial. Later in the episode, we hear him say that he contacted LabCorp, which had performed the tests on the blood in the vial, and LabCorp said "they don't do that" (poke holes in the rubber stopper). It is a "red-letter day" for the defense, he says.

Making a Murderer presents all of this in dramatic fashion. We do *not* hear that the hole in the top of the tube was actually made by a nurse when the blood was first collected from Steven Avery, not by some phantom police conspirator. *This is how all blood gets into collection tubes*, as you are probably aware if you have ever had blood drawn yourself. LabCorp would simply open the tube to get at the blood for testing, but to get the blood in there in the first place after drawing it from Steven Avery, nurse Marlene Kraintz poked a hole in the vacuum-fed tube with a needle. She swore out a statement to this effect, and would have testified at trial if required. However, once it became clear that the hole was standard and completely innocent, the defense abandoned the "hole as proof of tampering" angle, to the extent that her testimony wasn't needed at all. The filmmakers, of course, knew this, but chose to omit the innocent explanation—and leave the more exciting "red-letter day" tampering "proof" to stand instead.

Finally, in that same episode, a gleeful Jerry Buting tells the camera:

"So we looked around and one guy's name just kept coming up over and over and over every place we looked. At critical moments. And that was Lieutenant James Lenk.

"Lenk is the guy who finds the key in the bedroom on the seventh entry, supposedly in plain view. Lenk is deposed just three weeks before this Halbach disappearance. And then, most peculiar of all, is when we looked in Steven's old 1985 case file in the clerk's office. Some items from that court file ultimately proved to exonerate Steven. Interestingly enough, **the transmittal form that goes with the evidence in 2002 to the crime lab is filled out by none other than, at that time, Detective Sergeant James Lenk.** *And I said to myself, 'Whoa. This is starting to sound more than just coincidental.'"*

Innocence Project lawyers never asked for the Avery blood vial to be sent to the crime lab in 2002; only fingernail scrapings and hairs needed to be transported and tested. By 2002, Avery's DNA profile had already been developed by the lab, and therefore his blood didn't need to be sent to any lab again. This profile would be verified by a buccal swab taken of Avery in 2003 (a "buccal swab" is a noninvasive way of collecting a person's DNA, by swabbing the inside of their cheek with what looks like a Q-tip). In short, the suggestion that Lenk signed a transmittal form sending the vial of blood to the crime lab is simply untrue.

Things get a little legalistic here, but this evidence admissibility theory is important to understand, especially as it was glossed over in *Making a Murderer*. In Wisconsin, in order to advance a claim of third-party liability at trial—in other words, in order to present evidence that someone else committed the crime—the defense must have "some proof" that a *specific person* other than the charged defendant did a *specific thing* that shows a "legitimate tendency" to have committed the crime. If the defense only has a "hunch" or wants to use a vague "somebody else did it" defense, courts will exclude that from being presented to a jury. It's just not specific enough. The reason for this rule is obvious—no one, not even a defense attorney, should be allowed to accuse another citizen of criminal wrongdoing without at least "some proof."

Similarly, if the defense wants to offer "frame-up" evidence, they must identify specifically *who* planted the evidence, and demonstrate the direct connection that this person had to the evidence they allege was used to frame the defendant.

This is where the importance of the vial of blood in the clerk's office comes into sharp focus. The defense named Lenk and Colborn as the specific individuals who planted evidence, and therefore Lenk or Colborn needed to have a direct connection to the vial of blood in order to claim that vial was used to plant the blood in Teresa's car.

What was their motive? Although the defense never came out and accused either Lenk or Colborn of actually killing

Teresa Halbach, they refused to eliminate that as a possibility. Importantly, no evidence was ever presented that would tie either officer to Avery's case—remember, it was Lenk and Colborn's *lack* of connection to the Avery case that allowed their involvement in the search and investigation in the first place. Both had no involvement in the 1985 Beernsten assault case, as neither was even employed by Manitowoc County at the time. Other than Colborn transferring a call in 1995, and Lenk seeing that a report was written about that same call in 2003, there was no hint of any connection to Avery.

The best the defense could muster was a "general motive" to fabricate, the theory being that *any* Manitowoc cop would conspire to convict Avery in order to help their employer, the County of Manitowoc, avoid having to pay out any of the Avery lawsuit proceeds. But this supposed "institutional bias" motive, even had it existed, was not enough to allow the defense to admit either "third-party liability" or "frame-up" evidence. They still needed their "some proof"—some direct connection with Avery's blood.

The blood vial, as it turned out, provided what the defense needed to advance their "frame-up" claim: what judge Patrick Willis called "barely enough evidence" to allow the attorneys to move forward with their allegations of evidence planting. Judge Willis could have, and, I argued, should have, rejected both "third-party liability" and "frame-up" as possible defenses, because the existence of the blood vial was not "proof" of anything and did not constitute a direct connection to the evidence, *unless* the defense put the vial in the hands of Lenk or Colborn.

Just as he implied in Episode 4 of *Making a Murderer*, Buting alleged to the court, in writing and orally at the January 19th, 2007 motion hearing, that Lieutenant Lenk "knew" of the blood vial because "his name is on these [transmittal] documents in 2002." The defense theory was that Lenk "would have known" of the vial's existence, as illustrated by his signing the form when he transmitted the evidence to the lab in 2002. Makes sense, right?

What we all know now, and what I believe the defense knew all along, was that Lenk was *not* aware of the blood vial's existence. In *Making a Murderer*, the filmmakers cut to a 2002 "evidence transmittal" form, which bears the signature of Lt. James Lenk. Looking closer at the form shown in the episode, it clearly relates to the transmittal of "the hairs and fingernail scrapings," *which were housed separately*, only—there is no mention of the blood vial.

If Judge Willis had known that the blood vial was never touched by Lenk in 2002, I'm guessing the planting/frame-up defense would never have been allowed. If the truth about the "unsealed" evidence box had been presented—that it was unsealed as a result of prosecutors and defense attorneys jointly opening the box as part of Avery's rape case exoneration process—I'm guessing the planting/frame-up defense would never have been allowed. But Willis was led to believe the story of Lenk handling and transmitting the suspiciously unsealed blood vial. And the planting defense was allowed into the murder trial.

————————

Whiffs of conspiracy, black-bag jobs, and double-dealing permeated the air. The defense team argued that sheriff's deputies, who supposedly enjoyed secret access to the clerk's office, had removed the vial of blood, without any clerk's office employee noticing, perhaps in the dead of night. Those rogue officers, so the theory went, took the blood to the Avery salvage yard (or wherever the victim's SUV was located at the time). The defense had no evidence, they said, of where the SUV was being stashed, presumably in law enforcement custody, but maintained that the cops planted that same blood in six different places within Teresa's RAV4, thus manufacturing strong evidence against Steven Avery in the murder of Teresa Halbach. Like many unsubstantiated claims, this theory collapses under the most cursory scrutiny. (The vial appeared quite full, and yet somehow they had planted enough for six stains?) And, like every claim the defense advanced about police planting or misconduct, they had *zero evidence* it had ever occurred.

Still, when I first heard about the vial—on December 6th, 2006—I thought the defense case had gotten stronger. And given that the defense team had strategically waited until December 14th, 2006—the last day before the discovery deadline for all evidence sought to be introduced—to arrange joint examination of the vial and alert us of their intent to use it at trial, I was worried that we (the State) would have no real opportunity to test the sample before the trial began in February. The forensic science expert on our prosecution team, Milwaukee County ADA Norm

Gahn, was convinced the blood vial was crucial to Avery's defense, and if we could get the blood tested for the presence of EDTA, and compare it to the blood found in the victim's SUV, perhaps we could destroy the "planting" defense before the case got to the jury. I wasn't as sure, but I had so much trust and respect for Norm that I decided to let him handle this issue.

EDTA is a preservative and anticoagulant found in all "purple-topped" blood vials. It's the chemical compound that keeps the blood in liquid form for many years. The blood in the vial would of course have EDTA in it, and if the blood at the scene had been planted, it would as well. It followed, of course, that the jury would then know, unequivocally, whether the defendant's blood in the victim's vehicle had come from the clerk of court's purple-topped vial. If the blood in the vehicle did *not* contain EDTA, then it was clearly from Avery himself actively bleeding—and meant Avery had to have been inside the victim's SUV.

Believe it or not, the EDTA test was originally developed for the trial of O. J. Simpson. In that case, the testing protocol turned out to be flawed, as the lab suffered "carry-over" positive results from earlier samples tested, so no EDTA test results were ever admitted into evidence by Justice Lance Ito. After the O. J. trial, the problems with the testing were eliminated by making changes to the testing protocol, and the test was peer-reviewed in 1997 by the *Journal of Analytical Toxicology*. The problem was that the FBI, the only lab with a developed procedure to perform the test to detect the presence of EDTA, would likely need three to four months for the testing.

Of course, with O. J., *both* the State and defense had asked that EDTA testing be performed—the attorneys, on both sides, hoped to get to the truth about whether there was EDTA in the recovered Simpson blood. In contrast, on January 4th, 2007, Avery's defense duo told the court they had "no intention" of having the vial of blood tested for the presence of EDTA. Though they acknowledged that the presence of EDTA in the blood found in the RAV4 would prove their "planting" theory, they actively tried to prevent our testing by filing motions to block the release of the vial. They didn't *want* to know the results of the EDTA inquiry. They were banking on us not being able to come up with results in the first place, and inviting the jury to "speculate" what the results may have been.

But we did get our results. And so, in late February, when the trial was under way, the defense suddenly and crucially wanted EDTA testing of their own. They demanded the same delay for testing they had objected to when we asked for it. The best summation of the situation came from Judge Willis himself, who, after ruling that the FBI test results would be admissible, denied the defense request for a continuance so they could secure their own EDTA result (they had also argued that the public should pay for the private testing). On March 5th, 2007, Judge Willis said:

> *The defense has made the alleged planting of blood a vital part of this case. As defense counsel pointed out at the January 4 hearing, he, meaning Mr. Avery, has been saying from the beginning, to anybody with a microphone and TV camera,*

*initially as early as November 2005, that if his blood was
in the Toyota, somebody planted it. So there hasn't been any
secret about his defense and his view of the facts.*

*If testing of the blood was determined by the defense to be
vitally necessary to that planting defense, which was known
from the very beginning, it should have been pursued far earlier than it has been.*

*The bottom line in this case is that both parties had an
opportunity in this case to pursue testing. The court believes
that because of its earlier knowledge of the existence of the blood
vial . . . the defense had a slightly earlier opportunity, at least
than the State, but did not pursue the testing. And for that
reason a continuation of the trial at this point is not warranted.*

The defense hoped the State would not be able to show that
the blood vial contained EDTA, while the stains did not, thereby
proving that the stains could not have come from the blood in the
vial. They gambled, and they lost. They were willing to allege that
two cops—with no connection to the blood—were crooked, and
still it backfired. While *Making a Murderer* seemed to suggest the
EDTA test was rushed or experimental, neither is true. The FBI
has, in fact, published a report of the test's detection levels, and
both the FBI's chief of chemistry and an independent scientific
auditor have provided extensive testimony about its reliability.

Avery's blood, the DNA that helped establish his innocence in
2003, was now solid, incontrovertible evidence of his guilt.

CHAPTER SIX

The Key

For *Making a Murderer* conspiracy buffs, the ignition key for Teresa's RAV4 might be the piece of evidence that most convinces them that law enforcement officers framed an innocent man. A required ingredient in any recipe for an Avery setup, the "planted" key, and the circumstances surrounding its discovery, are for them proof of law enforcement corruption in the case. From my perspective, of course, the key represents something else entirely: another unimpeachable bar in Avery's jail cell door.

It's true. Sheriff's deputies did not find the key the first or second or even third time they entered the trailer. Avery partisans dub each entry a "search," which presumably is how they are able to claim the key wasn't found until the "sixth search." In truth, the key was found during the first complete and thorough search of Avery's bedroom.

On November 5th, the team of Sergeant Bill Tyson (of the Calumet County Sheriff's Department), Lieutenant James Lenk, Detective Dave Remiker, and Sergeant Andrew Colborn (all of the Manitowoc County Sheriff's Department), entered the residence for the first time, for an initial sweep. They weren't searching for evidence then; they were looking for signs of Teresa Halbach, or for Teresa herself, dead or alive. Ten minutes later, they walked out empty-handed. "What struck me was how clean it was," Lenk recalls. "Not just clean, but freshly cleaned and smelling of recently shampooed carpets."

Later that evening, officers began their first real search of the trailer. Night fell and thunderstorms thrashed through. Fatigue became a factor. Tom Fassbender decided to call off the search before it was completed. Nobody intended that the trailer would be gone over only once. On the issue of that first night's search, and its incompleteness, let's allow the Wisconsin Court of Appeals, which examined the issue, to sum up:

> *Fassbender testified that most of the investigators in the trailer had already been working for twelve hours or more and exhaustion and safety issues were becoming factors that could affect the searchers' ability to locate and collect evidence. In addition, there was "a horrendous rainstorm going on" that created a risk of evidence being destroyed or lost as officers went in and out of the trailer to get equipment. Thus, the officers were focused on looking for the type of evidence that would be most at risk of being destroyed under those*

conditions. Fassbender testified that in debriefing the officers that night, he was telling people: "[W]e are not done in that house." Fassbender testified, as of Saturday night, the trailer "was still part of my scene. This is an ongoing search."

Tom Fassbender, Mark Wiegert, and I, after each long day of the ongoing investigation, would meet and "debrief" with other key investigative members, making to-do lists and planning the next day's search efforts. We sent officers back into Avery's trailer three times to recover (seize) specific items of personal property we believed had evidentiary value—but never to "search" the trailer.

Nor were the other entries made during the first three days of the investigation considered "searches" by anyone involved. On November 6th, the trailer was entered twice. Officers went in once to retrieve specifically listed items that had been noticed the night before—including a vacuum cleaner and guns—and were in the trailer for twenty minutes. That same day, techs from the state crime lab entered to look for DNA evidence with reactive lighting and to take swabs. Then, on November 7th, there was a seven-minute entry solely for the purpose of recording the serial number from Avery's computer—nobody entered the bedroom.

On November 8th, officers were at last sent in to complete the trailer search that had been called off on the night of November 5th. Fassbender told Colborn to search the bedroom furniture and recover the large number of pornographic photos Avery had collected of his former wife and girlfriend. This, then, is when the key was discovered. Sixth entry: first search, or a continuation of it. If you want to split hairs, I suppose you could call it the second search—but it was the first thorough search of the bedroom furniture.

Colborn says, "Those first entries were very targeted, with one of the lead investigators telling us to go retrieve the computer, or the guns, or the ammunition, or specific documents on Avery's desk, but it wasn't until November 8th that we were instructed, for the first time, to complete a thorough search of all the rooms and furniture."

Colborn has been pummeled on this issue. Fellow law enforcement officials have grilled him. The prosecution team pressed him, as did the defense attorneys. And finally, he's been battered and hung out to dry by media—including *Making a Murderer*—questioning how such a crucial piece of physical evidence simply "appeared" on the Avery bedroom carpet during that much-scrutinized search.

Clear, unapologetic, never wavering—that was the nature of Andy Colborn's explanation. What he told Fassbender on November 8th, 2005, matched what he told me when I interviewed him for this book in June of 2016:

"On November 8th, Lieutenant Lenk, Officer Kucharski, and myself were assigned to search the Avery trailer one last time. Although we had been in there on several occasions the previous three days, we had not been asked to go room by room, and through all the furniture, looking for evidence. As I was removing items from a small bookcase against the bedroom wall, I had become increasingly frustrated with the task, and with the porn photos of his former wives and girlfriends I was sorting through.

"While I was putting photo albums and other items back into the cabinet, I was none too gentle, and was slamming them in there pretty good. I had moved the bookcase and was shaking it rather strongly, and then moved the piece of furniture back to its original location. It was then that Lenk said, 'There's a key!' I swear it wasn't there just a minute before, and I realized it must have been hidden inside or behind the small bookcase I had just moved."

Lenk recalls "seeing the key just sitting there on the carpet. I knew Andy had been kind of rough with the bookcase, and figured it just fell out. I had no idea what kind of key it was until Andy noticed it had a Toyota emblem on it. I still didn't connect it to Teresa's SUV, as I'm kind of embarrassed to admit that I didn't really know a RAV4 was made by Toyota. Andy and Kucharski knew it right away, though."

The famous bookcase in Avery's bedroom was seized during the investigation, and clearly visible was the half-inch gap between the interior shelf and the back panel of the cabinet. The jury was shown how the key could easily fall from the back corner of the shelf, down the back of the cabinet, and "appear" on the carpet when the bookcase was handled roughly. See for yourself in the following photos. No "magic" required—just gravity.

The bookshelf before it was moved

Back of the bookshelf, showing gap

All of this was explained at trial, but the explanation didn't appear in *Making a Murderer*. Instead, Officer Kucharski's testimony was shown—spliced.

Sometimes we saw answers from direct examination spliced in after questions from cross-examination. Most significantly, at one point Kucharski is asked if he knows how the key "got there" (on the floor), and he says "yes," going on to give a detailed explanation and discuss the broken bookshelf. None of this is shown in the documentary. Instead, we see only his testimony that Lenk "pointed to the floor and said 'there's a key there.'" I mean, hey, that *does* sound suspicious. It is hard to fault viewers for thinking so, when they weren't given the whole story.

Many ask why Avery would keep Teresa's car key. Why not just toss it into the burn barrel with her camera and phone instead of leaving it around for the cops to find? In my view, it's because Avery still needed the SUV to be operable. The car crusher on the Avery salvage yard, where Avery intended to pulverize Teresa's car to eliminate it as a source of evidence, was located in the farthest corner from his trailer, but relatively close to where he had stashed the SUV—just not close enough to push it or use the forklift. It would need to be driven to the crusher.

If citizen searches hadn't stumbled on the RAV4 on November 5th, while Avery was up north at the family's Crivitz cottage, that's exactly what he would have done, perhaps as early as that afternoon. He told Jodi that he intended to come back from the cottage that Saturday afternoon, alone. Crushing a car is not something that can be done discreetly, and it's not like such a steady stream of cars were being crushed that Steve could slip Teresa's in unnoticed. With the rest of the family away in Crivitz, Avery would at last have had the opportunity to crush the car, unseen by any witnesses. Unfortunately for him, Steve had no way to predict that his brother, Earl Avery, when asked, would give citizen searchers free range over Avery Salvage. The salvage lot was private property, and if Earl hadn't given permission, Pam Sturm would never have found Teresa's car that day. Steve could have crushed the car that afternoon, and probably would have gotten away with murder.

It is hard not to see this moment as a significant one, not just for Steve, but for the Avery family as a whole. The Averys stick together—they keep each other's secrets, and distrust of law enforcement is a pillar of the family code. Earl couldn't have known it, but on that cloudy November morning, he loosed the bonds that had served and preserved the Avery clan for generations, and the troubled family would never quite regain its former unity.

———————

The key found in Steven Avery's bedroom was photographed, processed, and rushed to the Madison crime lab for analysis the same day it was discovered. It was indeed Teresa's key—not only did it fit her ignition, it still had the blue fob attached, which perfectly fit the blue lanyard with the National Guard logo, the one

Teresa's sister Katie had obtained for her big sister, recovered by the crime lab from inside the RAV4's center console.

Perhaps most importantly, state crime lab unit chief Sherry Culhane developed a "full nuclear DNA profile" from DNA found on the key. It was, Culhane testified, "non-blood" DNA matching Steven Avery. Why is that important? Well, the cops were only alleged to be walking around with a vial of Avery's blood, not his skin cells. Avery handled this key. It was Teresa's, and obviously needed by Steven to later crush the vehicle, parked and camouflaged in the opposite corner of the salvage yard. It was found in Avery's bedroom, still attached to the blue fob, covered with skin cells sloughed from Avery's sweaty hands—this is what cops, prosecutors, and the rest of the critical thinking world refers to as a "game changer." How did the defense intend to explain away the defendant's own DNA on the key?

They didn't, unless another vague cry of "it was planted" counts as an explanation. Because Teresa Halbach's DNA was *not* on the key, the defense and internet crime enthusiasts—including, most recently, Avery's new attorney, Kathleen Zellner—argue that Avery's skin cells "must have" been planted there, and assert that having only one DNA profile recovered from the key was very suspicious.

Sherry Culhane, the only expert who was asked about this subject, quickly put the conspiracy theory to rest during Avery's jury trial. On cross-examination by attorney Buting, here's what Culhane told the jury:

Buting: Now, you found no mixture of DNA on that key, right?

Culhane: Right.

Buting: You did not find any DNA of Teresa Halbach on that key, did you?

Culhane: That's correct . . .

Buting: . . . Now, there are some studies in the Wickenheiser report, for instance, that talk about how the last person who touches an item may leave the major portion of DNA that's left on there?

Culhane: Yes.

Buting: But most often when that happens, there's still a mixture and there's a minor contributor as well, right?

Culhane: No, I-I would disagree with that. In some cases, yes. It's very difficult. There's no way to really predict that. If you have someone who's a good shedder, and sheds a lot of DNA, when they touch something, a lot of studies show that—the last person is going to be the DNA you pick up.

This didn't stop *Making a Murderer* from showcasing the defense theory—that only Steve's DNA appearing on the key was suspicious—*without* including the explanation from Ms. Culhane. "Planting" is surely more complicated and improbable than the possibility, for example, that Avery got blood on the key from his cut finger and then washed the blood off the key before stashing it away for later use. Washing it off would have removed not only the blood but Teresa's DNA, while his skin cells would have been left behind again when he hid it. Even if you're hiding a key and don't plan on anyone finding it, you might decide washing visible blood off it first isn't a bad idea. And, of course, drops of Steve's blood were found near the bathroom sink in his trailer.

———————

In the end, one of the best defenses against allegations that the key was planted is simple common sense. The fact that Colborn and Lenk are the ones who found the key is clearly *inconsistent* with the key having been planted at all. Put yourself in a corrupt cop's shoes, just for a moment. If you're a crooked cop willing to plant evidence to ensure a murder conviction against Steven Avery, wouldn't you make sure as hell *you* weren't the law enforcement officer who "found" the key? Colborn and Lenk knew all Manitowoc officers at the scene were under extra scrutiny. If they'd planted the key, they would also have ensured Officer Kucharski, the non-Manitowoc team leader, was the one to find it—it's not like this would have been difficult to arrange. Any cop smart enough to set a man up for murder, under the nose of all of those experienced investigators, would certainly be smart enough to know that he should not find the planted evidence himself.

Never deterred by common sense, Buting continued to push the claim that the key was planted. His thinking, as stated in the

Netflix series, was, "If we can get them to believe the key was planted, anything is possible." The defense seemed to believe that if they could get the jury to accept that one piece of evidence was put there by law enforcement, the jury would be willing to believe *all* the evidence was planted—that Steven Avery had been framed. And the jury, whether the judge had allowed "frame-up" evidence or not, already knew that this was Avery's defense. Avery himself had been talking about "planted evidence" on the news *even before evidence linking him to the crime was found*. His defense team spent months before the trial publicizing their client's "frame-up" version of events. The jury knew all about these allegations without Avery ever having to testify. He never had to say one word, or be subject to cross-examination, or have the jury weigh the credibility of his testimony. His version of the story had been told on the news well before this case ever made it to the courtroom. It makes it difficult to agree with the defense conclusion that the criminal justice system was heavily biased in favor of the prosecution, and against poor, defenseless Steven Avery.

Here, though, comes the most important consideration of all. This key was not simply a random "Toyota key," the phrase used so often in the defense's cross-examination, or a "spare key," the phrase used by Kathleen Zellner. This was not even just a key made to fit the victim's SUV ignition. This was *Teresa's* key, with the other half of *her* lanyard attached, the lanyard that was in the center console of the locked SUV, inside the secure Madison crime lab. This was the key that Teresa had with her. It had not been burned. It had Avery's DNA on it. Until November 3rd, no one knew for sure that Avery had been Teresa's last stop before she disappeared—remember, until late in the day on November 3rd, Avery himself was claiming that Teresa had "not shown up" for her appointment that Halloween day.

So, if you believe the key was planted in Steven Avery's trailer, you must be willing to believe activities far more sinister occurred as well. Are you willing to believe that, sometime between November 3rd and November 5th, officers discovered a crime scene—perhaps Teresa's bloody car with the key still inside it—and then moved everything to Avery's property? Are you willing to believe that these officers found Teresa before her body was burned, hid the crime, and kept the key? Are you willing to believe that they were the ones to burn and chop up her body? That they killed her themselves? How far are you willing to take this? How thoroughly are you willing to suspend common sense to explain away the evidence?

CHAPTER SEVEN

The Bones

For me, the spring of 2006 was primarily the Spring of Steven Avery, a season dedicated to trial preparation. But Avery and Dassey didn't occupy my every moment—I had other obligations too. I was a father to a high school senior, Andy, who played tennis and basketball (I coached) and wanted a career as an entrepreneur. I had been the primary custodial parent since Andy's mother and I divorced twelve years earlier, in 1994.

Like most Wisconsin parents, I prided myself on not missing any of my child's matches or games. The University of Wisconsin–Whitewater accepted Andy, and he prepared to head to college that August. I took him to play in his first poker tournament in Michigan, after his eighteenth birthday, forty-eight hours after the Brendan Dassey confession bombshell rocked the Halbach murder case.

In a sense, we'd studied together. While Andy pored over college applications—that modern-day bête noire—I, again, focused
on forensics, on science. Not blood this time. This time, the most
challenging and important subject for me was the science of
bones. Was I back in high school again?

Not with Leslie around.

Forensic anthropologist Leslie Eisenberg is the smartest
woman I know. A graduate of New York University, she spent her
days in Wisconsin analyzing bones and other human remains—
mostly involving Native American burial sites—and being
regarded as one of the nation's very best bone experts. Officials
called upon her to assist in national tragedies like the World Trade
Center attack in 2001 and Hurricane Katrina, when identification of human remains became an increasingly in-demand scientific specialty.

And so, with one of the nation's best within our state borders,
it was Leslie Eisenberg whom I asked to identify hundreds of tiny
pieces of bone fragment—some so brittle that if handled they
would instantly break apart—and determine if they were human,
came from one body, were found in the same place, and whether
they were burned. And her most important assignment of all: to
tell us, if she could, how Teresa Halbach was killed.

Under Dr. Eisenberg's direction in a large storage building
at the Wisconsin Crime Lab, with scaffolding and tarps set up
like makeshift banquet tables, DCI arson investigators and law
enforcement officers from Calumet County sorted the recovered
burn pit material. Later, as she walked me through the process of

sorting and identifying the bones, I shook my head in bewilderment. Eisenberg smiled and said, "It looks likes a lot, but it's not as hard as it seems, at least not for me."

There were pieces from nearly every bone in the human body.

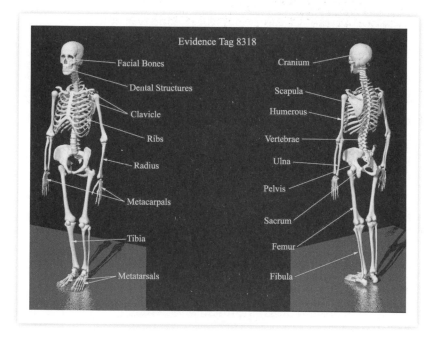

Chart showing recovered and identified bone pieces

Some of the fragments were the size of a poker chip, others as small as a sliver. All were painstakingly analyzed. Eisenberg testified that those bones belonged to a female, no older than thirty to thirty-five years of age.

By reviewing the heavy charring of the bone material, and the extent to which those bones were mutilated through mechanical chopping and breaking, she determined that they were cut and burned in an obvious attempt to thwart detection and identification. Whoever did it didn't want this young woman found.

Against all odds, one femur bone that Eisenberg examined still had muscle tissue attached. Somehow, the intense heat hadn't incinerated it. DNA expert Sherry Culhane was able to conclude that the tissue belonged to Teresa.

Leslie Eisenberg also examined two skull fragments. They told another macabre story. Before Teresa's body was burned, Leslie found, Teresa was shot in the head, once in the parietal region (near the left temple) and once in the occipital region (the back of the skull). Each skull fragment had a "defect," with the skull material itself "beveled," creating the unmistakable sign of a bullet entry wound. With the assistance of state crime lab element specialist Ken Olson, the skull fragments were X-rayed, using highly sensitive mammography film. Tiny particles of lead were detected, particles left behind by a bullet entering the victim's skull. Cause of death: homicidal violence. Manner of death: gunshot.

On the important, and hotly contested, issue of the primary burn site, Dr. Eisenberg was confident. Of course, if you've ever spoken to a scientist, you know they aren't in the habit of making definite pronouncements, but Dr. Eisenberg regarded it as "extremely unlikely" that the primary burn site had been anywhere but the burn pit behind Avery's garage. Department of Justice attorney Tom Fallon questioned Dr. Eisenberg at trial:

Fallon: Now, you did offer an opinion that you believe the location for the primary burning episode here was the burn pit behind the garage; is that correct?

Eisenberg: That is correct.

Fallon: Would you please elaborate for us your reasoning on that?

Eisenberg: Number one, in the order of priority, would be that the overwhelming majority of fragments, burned fragments that were identified by me as human, were found in that location behind the garage, in and adjacent to the burn pit, that there were, in my opinion, many small, delicate, brittle fragments that would have been left behind someplace else had that not been the primary burn location. And if that had been the case, I would have been able to recognize those fragments from another location and did not, except for burn barrel number two. And that all the human bone fragments that were fragmented and badly burned from that location show . . . approximately the same degree of charring, burning, and calcination variously throughout the material recovered in the burn pit and adjacent areas.

Fallon: Since you have concluded that the burn pit was the location of the primary burning episode, tell us why, in your opinion, burn barrel number two [*the barrel behind Dassey's residence*] would not have been?

Eisenberg: I believe that burn barrel number two would not have been the primary burn location because I would have expected to find more bone fragments that I would have been able to—bone fragments, and human bone fragments, and dental structures—that I would have been able to identify as human in burn barrel number two than actually I was—than actually were found . . .

Some of the pieces of bone found at the burn pit were smaller than your pinky nail. Some of the bones had likely been reduced entirely to ash. Tiny rivets were found, a zipper, tooth fragments. The four bone pieces in the burn barrel were, in general, larger pieces than those found in the burn pit. I believe the most likely explanation is that Avery moved four of the larger pieces of bone that were not breaking down as well to the barrel, perhaps to burn and break them down further. Lest you think there was any great danger in these pieces being recognized in one of the barrels, they were still small, maybe an inch and a half, and nothing that would have looked out of the ordinary in a barrel that already contained animal bones, a barrel used to burn garbage and belonging to a family of avid hunters.

Fallon: . . . Given the nature and condition of the char-ring, the calcine defect on these bones, does it take a professional such as yourself to be able to clearly identify human from nonhuman burned bone?

Eisenberg: I would say yes, except when nonhuman bone is of a size, and intact, that someone might recognize a bone or some other nonhuman bone. But, yes, I would agree with you, given the charring, and burning, and calcination of the fragments, in fact, the majority of the contents of the burn pit and adjacent area, that, yes, it would take someone who has experience looking and identifying human from nonhuman bone fragments.

Fallon: Would you say the same for what was found in burn barrel number two?

Eisenberg: Yes, I would.

───────────

Eisenberg wasn't the only person to testify as to the location of the primary burn site. Special Agent Rodney Pevytoe, of the Arson Bureau at the Wisconsin Department of Justice, had been viewing burn sites for thirty years, earning him the reputation of being the most experienced arson investigator in the state. He too believed that Teresa had been burned in the pit behind Avery's garage.

Pevytoe also explained more about the fire itself. Tires, he felt, accelerated it. A van seat had also been burned, a van seat with padding made of polyurethane foam, referred to as "solid gasoline." Accelerated this way, a fire could burn a body to bone and ash in a matter of hours.

Pevytoe also found tangled masses of steel wire in the burn pit, the remnants of steel-belted radial tires. He testified that bone fragments were deeply intertwined in the wire "to the point where I actually had to physically pull apart the wire to get in there."

Significance? Bones and the tires were burned together—no sinister team of law enforcement conspirators could have simply dumped a mass of bone fragments onto the ashes of Steven Avery's innocent tire fire. What's more, tiny steel fragments from the wires were found in the soil of the burn pit itself, and that soil was black and oily, indicating, according to the arson investigator, that it had been the site of a tire fire. A rake with bits of the steel from the tires still caught in its teeth was found nearby, along with other implements used to stoke the fire and break up the bones.

———————

The defense couldn't produce much in response. They brought up three bone fragments found in a quarry nearby, which Eisenberg thought could possibly be human pelvic bone, but could not be sure were not animal bones after all. Many other bones, determined to be animal bones, were found at the quarry, which was part of an area hunting site. If the pelvis bones *were* human, and *were* Teresa's, it doesn't take much imagination to come up with possible explanations, including that Avery threw a few of the larger bone pieces there, where there were already animal bones, in hopes of concealing them; or something as innocent as an animal taking one of the bones from the burn pit area and carrying it to the nearby quarry. To be crystal clear, there was nothing at all to suggest the quarry had been the primary burn site—nothing.

The defense's forensic anthropologist, Dr. Scott Fairgrieve, never visited the burn site, never examined the bones, and worked entirely from pictures provided by the defense attorneys—this isn't so unusual for expert witnesses testifying in a limited capacity, but while this was explained to the jury, it was never mentioned in *Making a Murderer*. On the stand, Fairgrieve agreed with my friend Leslie Eisenberg's findings on just about everything.

His one point of disagreement, out of which the defense tried and failed to make something, was his unwillingness to identify the primary burn site. However, he did *not* go so far as to say he thought the Avery burn pit was *not* the primary burn site, only that, based upon the pictures he was shown, he could not make a determination about the primary burn site, and that in his prior experience, when bones were moved, the majority of the bones were found in the location they were moved *to*, not the location they were moved *from*. In reality, if you read the transcripts, you will see that the defense expert explicitly declined to offer any opinion about the location of the primary burn site in this case at all.

Pay attention now, because you are about to hear one of the most willfully misleading arguments the defense made in the entire case. Teresa's bones were found in at least two places— bones from various parts of her skeleton. Therefore, obviously, some of the bones were moved after or during burning. So far, so good. However, the defense wanted the jury to believe that because, according to their expert, in most cases where bones are moved, the majority of bones are found where they are moved *to* and not where they were moved *from*, the fact that the majority of Teresa's bones were found in the burn pit meant that they were moved *to* that location *from* somewhere else.

Well, in most cases where bones are moved, it makes *perfect sense* that most of the bones would be found where they were moved to. Think about it: if you kill someone, and you burn their bones, and then decide to move them in an attempt to conceal your crime, you're probably going to try to move *all* the bones, or at least as many as you possibly can. This is just good sense, as a murderer! However, Teresa's isn't really a case where "the bones were moved." This is a case where *a few* bones were moved, maybe to try to speed up the destruction process, maybe to get rid of some pieces that were not breaking down as well. There is no evidence that ANY attempt was made to move the majority of the bones. So a statement about "most cases where the bones are moved" from an expert speaking generally about his experience isn't applicable here. Despite this, the defense expert's testimony was presented in *Making a Murderer* as some sort of bombshell.

―――――――

And of course, as mentioned earlier in this book, though never once referenced in *Making a Murderer*, the contents of Teresa Halbach's purse—her cell phone, camera, and PDA—were found in Steven's own burn barrel. Another of Steven Avery's nephews, Brendan's seventeen-year-old brother, Blaine, saw his uncle Steve place a white plastic garbage bag into his burn barrel, approximately twenty feet to the north and east of his front door, on the afternoon of October 31st, and then observed smoke and the telltale signs of active burning. Another witness, a friend of Earl Avery's, Robert Fabian, saw a fire coming from that same burn barrel that afternoon and smelled burning plastic.

No cop could stand over the burn barrel, stoking it and putting tires and other flammables in it while the electronics burned, without *someone* seeing them. Someone, two someones, *did* see Steven. Why should we ignore the testimony of these witnesses? Why should we discount the testimony of experts, from different agencies and different disciplines, who agree that Teresa was burned at the burn pit behind Steven Avery's garage? Grim and plain—that was the nature of these truths. They may not be as exciting as conspiracy theories, but they do have the virtue of being supported by facts.

CHAPTER EIGHT

The Bullet

Immediately after Brendan Dassey confessed to Wiegert and Fassbender on March 1st, 2006, my favorite two officers briefed me. Search warrant in hand, we headed to Mishicot, taking our now-familiar route to the Avery salvage property. Never had we considered the garage there as the murder scene. Now, potentially, it was—and it might even make the case for us, with more physical evidence—whether Dassey testified against Uncle Steve or not.

Snow still lay thickly over the yard that evening, great dunes of it rising out of the dark. Given the ground cover, it'd be easy to find fresh footprints. Officers shoveled snowdrifts from around the garage entry doors—the large double door at the front of the building, and the smaller access door to the right. Watching, I thought any "planting" allegations that might be raised could be silenced with a photo taken at that moment—with no footprints in the snow, bad actors, if they existed, would have had to fly over the white stuff to make mischief inside this garage.

Portable floodlights illuminated the interior, which was filled with shit—Steve's shit: tools, gas cans, lawn mowers, painting supplies, and rusted junk sat in sloppy piles. Teresa Halbach died here, according to Brendan. I was convinced, and Mark and Tom agreed, that evidence of her murder lurked therein. Amid the shit.

With Avery's detritus removed from the garage, officers jack-hammered chunks of concrete out of its floor, looking for blood that might have soaked through the cracks. Unlikely they'd find any, I thought. From the beginning, I'd theorized that Steven put down a tarp on which to lay Teresa.

My theory remained viable. The concrete floor reacted to the chemical Luminol, which glows under black light to indicate the presence of blood on surfaces. But Luminol doesn't just detect the presence of human blood—its neon glow is also triggered by animal blood, some bleaches, and metals. Analysts did follow-up tests to more precisely identify the substance as human blood, but in this case those tests came back inconclusive. No expert would be willing to testify that blood was present in Avery's garage in great quantities.

The only thing we could say for sure was that the garage floor had been cleaned with heavy applications of bleach and paint thinner, containers of which had been found earlier in the investigation—the substances identified by our new key witness, Brendan Dassey, as having been used on October 31st, 2005, to scrub the garage floor. The jeans he'd worn that night showed splash patterns from the bleach.

The most important pieces of evidence to come out of this garage search, it turned out, were bullets—more precisely, two bullet fragments. Special Agent Kevin Heimerl, a young DCI investigator, had been assigned the responsibility of coordinating the search of the garage that evening. He would testify at trial that one bullet fragment had been located in a crack in the garage's cement floor, flattened until it resembled the head of a roofing nail. It was too deformed to be of much use, held no DNA, and couldn't be matched to any specific gun.

The second bullet told a different tale. As he would tell the jury, Heimerl discovered this bullet while on his hands and knees, as he shined his flashlight under the large green air compressor at the back wall of the garage. It was "almost intact," and he carefully recovered the object, placing it in a small evidence box for later processing at the lab. It would be shown to bear traces of Teresa Halbach's DNA. This was the forensic discovery I had hoped for—physical evidence tying Steven Avery to Teresa's murder. This bullet would make the case.

On the witness stand a year later, state crime lab firearms expert Bill Newhouse testified that this bullet had been fired from Steven Avery's rifle, the one found hanging over his bed, using ammunition found in his scuffed desk drawers, to the exclusion of all other firearms and ammunition in the world.

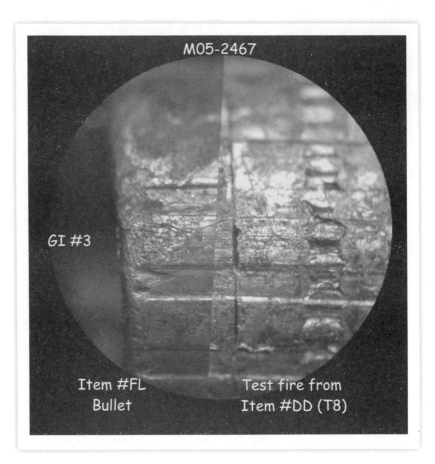

Magnified photo of the bullet compared to a test shot
from Avery's rifle—it's a match

Department of justice attorney Tom Fallon: Let's direct
your attention, then, to the remaining bullet, Item FL,
Exhibit No. 277; were you able to conduct an analysis of
that particular bullet?

Newhouse: I did.

Fallon: And were you able to make a determination as to whether Exhibit 277, bullet designation FL, was fired from the Marlin Glenfield .22 caliber rifle in front of you?

Newhouse: Yes, I was.

Fallon: And what conclusion were you able to reach?

Newhouse: In this case, I was able to be more specific. And, in fact, because of markings on the bullet in State's Exhibit 277, I was able to conclude that this bullet had been fired from this specific gun.

Fallon: All right. So Exhibit 277 had been fired from Exhibit 247?

Newhouse: That's correct.

Newhouse went on to describe the identical striations— grooves and scratches—found on the bullet recovered from the garage and test bullets fired from the rifle recovered from above Steven Avery's bed. These identical markings were so distinctive, and there were so many of them, that they could not be present on two bullets fired from different guns.

Fallon: All right. Is there—Does that mean it could not have been fired from any other gun?

Newhouse: It does.

Fallon: The opinion that Exhibit 277, item designation FL, was fired from Exhibit 247, the Marlin Glenfield, Model 60, .22 caliber rifle; do you hold that opinion to a reasonable degree of scientific certainty?

Newhouse: I do.

Fallon: The opinion that it could not have been fired from any other gun; do you hold that opinion to a reasonable degree of scientific certainty?

Newhouse: I do.

This testimony, concerning one of the most critical pieces of physical evidence tying Avery to Halbach's killing—testimony certainly considered by the jury—was never shown in *Making a Murderer*.

Naturally, the defense argued that the bullet had been planted. Avery's rifle was locked up in the state crime lab in Madison by the time the bullet was found, but surely, so the conspiracy theorist argument went, police could have picked up a bullet from the ground somewhere and planted it in the garage. After all, the Averys were hunters and gun enthusiasts; spent shell casings and bullets littered the property. Most of those, however, came from other guns, including other .22 caliber rifles, with bullets that could not be distinguished from those shot from Steve's .22 without help from the crime lab. It would have been a stroke of extraordinary luck to find a bullet that would later, upon microscopic examination, prove to have been shot from the rifle hanging above Avery's bed. And then, of course, there was the victim's DNA.

Finding a bullet in Avery's garage shot from his gun would hardly have been earth-shattering, but this particular bullet had passed through the body of Teresa Halbach. She'd been murdered in that garage, shot by Avery's rifle.

On February 23rd, 2007, Wisconsin State Crime Lab DNA expert Sherry Culhane testified that in order to remove any residual DNA from the bullet for testing, she "washed it," meaning she placed the bullet in a test tube with a solution designed to extract DNA. She then compared the DNA profile developed from the DNA on the bullet with the profile obtained from a sample residing in Teresa Halbach's medical record—specifically, a pap smear, kept securely at the hospital. It was a match. The source of the DNA on the bullet was Teresa Halbach.

In his closing argument, Jerry Buting told the jury that the DNA evidence was "contaminated" and asked them to ignore it. In truth, Sherry Culhane inadvertently introduced her own DNA into the "control sample" during the DNA testing. This type of error has no impact on the results of the test itself, but lab protocol would normally be to redo the test in its entirety. Unfortunately, because the DNA recovered on the bullet was in such a small quantity, the lab did not have the luxury of rewashing the bullet and starting over. The defense was given the option of retesting the bullet DNA themselves, but chose not to—they preferred to simply complain about lab protocol.

To be clear, NO contamination occurred on the bullet itself, or the sample taken from the bullet—just the control sample, a solution without any DNA that is used as a comparison. *Making a Murderer* gave plenty of time to Buting's accusations of contamination, but did not include the part of Culhane's testimony in which, while being questioned by prosecutor Norm Gahn, she explained why the control sample results had nothing to do with whether Teresa Halbach was the source of the DNA on the bullet:

Culhane: That means that during the extraction procedure I inadvertently introduced my own DNA into the negative control.

Gahn: Did that have any impact on your interpretation of your results?

Culhane: It did not have any impact as far as the profile from the evidence sample. It's just the fact that I introduced my own DNA into the manipulation control.

Gahn: Were there any other profiles developed on the bullet besides Teresa Halbach?

Culhane: No.

Gahn: Was Teresa Halbach's profile the only profile that you found on that bullet?

Culhane: Yes.

Gahn: Were there any mixtures?

Culhane: No.

Gahn: And your profile was found where?

Culhane: In the negative control, which should have had just reagents in it. It should not have had any DNA at all in it.

Gahn: How do you think your DNA profile got into that control?

Culhane: I believe my DNA profile was introduced during the time when I was setting up test samples; I was training two analysts, newer analysts, in the lab. And they were watching me. This sample was not an average sample, simply because we handled it a little different. It wasn't a swabbing and it wasn't a cutting. The washing part of it was a little bit different than what we usually do.

So I was explaining to them what I was doing and as I was setting it up. And apparently—I felt as if I was far enough away from my workbench not to introduce my DNA, but apparently I was incorrect.

Gahn: Now, your DNA did not come up on the bullet, did it?

Culhane: No.

Gahn: It only was in the control?

Culhane: That's correct.

Gahn: Do you have an opinion, to a reasonable degree of scientific certainty, whether Teresa Halbach is the source of the DNA on Item FL, the bullet?

Culhane: Yes.

Gahn: And what is that opinion?

Culhane: I believe she is the source of the DNA on that bullet.

While cops finished up in the garage, Fassbender and Wiegert searched the trailer where Barb Janda and Brendan Dassey lived. They found a pair of pink fur-lined handcuffs and leg irons, purchased by Barb on October 9th, 2005, while shopping with her brother Steven. Steven had bought a pair of new silver handcuffs and leg irons himself that day, a set that would be recovered from his trailer in November. There's nothing illegal about silver handcuffs, of course, and Teresa's DNA wasn't found on them, though it might seem a bit odd to some to be buying restraints when your girlfriend is in jail and expected to remain there for another six months.

Jodi Stachowski herself expressed surprise when learning Avery had purchased the items on October 9th. In a recorded jail call, she asked Avery who they were meant to be used with. "They were a surprise for my new wife," Steven insisted, trying to convince his imprisoned fiancée that he was thinking ahead almost six months to celebrating her release date.

Barb told Fassbender that sometime before October 31st, she and Steve argued about putting her van in the *Auto Trader* magazine, because she "really had no desire to sell it." Tom said, "Steve told Barb that he would take care of placing the ad, would arrange for the photographer to take the picture, and would even pay the fee for the photographer to come out and take the pictures for the magazine." Avery needed a reason to get Teresa to the salvage property on October 31st, and he couldn't do it the same way he did on October 10th.

The morning of October 10th, the day after he purchased the handcuffs and leg irons, Steven Avery summoned Teresa to the salvage property for a "hustle shot," simply meaning the photo shoot request came directly to the photographer from the customer, not through *Auto Trader* magazine.

October 10th is the date Avery is said to have greeted Teresa wearing only a white towel. Dean Strang theorized that Avery had come from a swim in his backyard kiddie pool that day, nothing untoward about it. The National Weather Service records indicate forty-six degrees as the high temperature on October 10th, 2005, in Mishicot—hardly swimming weather, even for Wisconsinites. The 10th of October is also the date Avery took digital photos of his erect penis, found date stamped and printed on his desk during the search of his trailer.

"It seems Teresa's last visit to the Avery property had a major impact on Steven," said Tom, dryly.

CHAPTER NINE

The Accomplice

Making a Murderer viewers can't forget Brendan Dassey, or help but feel sorry for him. He's the shuffling, mumbling young man with bad skin and broken-bowl haircut, a cipher adrift with tiny promise of a future. Heartbreakingly aware of his intellectual limitations, he says, "I'm stupid, Mom" to his mother, Barb, in a jailhouse call, prompting her lament: "You're not stupid to me."

During one of six interviews with investigators in which he implicates himself in the murder of Teresa Halbach, Brendan, a high school sophomore, asks, "How long is this gonna take? I have a project due in sixth hour." If you watched Making a Murderer, you heard that and shook your head, forlornly. Textbook example here, you thought, of unscrupulous investigators leading a suggestible and vulnerable teenager to confess to a crime he'd later swear he didn't actually commit.

Before Brendan's confession, I had no reason to believe that anyone other than Steven Avery had been involved in Teresa's murder—certainly not any of the minor children living on the compound. I never made Brendan Dassey as a killer, or even an accomplice. I never even ordered the collection of his DNA, as I had for the other, adult, members of the Avery clan. Did I underestimate him, or simply look right past him, as I assume has happened most of his life?

Interestingly, it wasn't a statement from Brendan Dassey himself that made us take a second look at him. Brendan's fourteen-year-old cousin, Kayla, the daughter of Earl and Candy Avery, told investigators in late February of 2006 that she was worried about Brendan. He'd lost forty pounds, she said, and had been crying uncontrollably. She said he'd seen something the night of the murder.

What we didn't know at the time—and what was never shown in *Making a Murderer*—was that Kayla had approached a school counselor the month before, in January, saying that she was scared to go over to the "shop" at her uncle's place. She'd also asked the counselor whether blood could "come up through concrete." Crucially, Kayla made these statements before investigators regarded the garage as a crime scene. None of this information was reported to authorities until after Brendan's arrest.

————————————

On February 27th, 2006, when the two investigators traveled to Mishicot High School to talk to Brendan, he remained a potential witness, not a suspect. Fassbender and Wiegert hoped to fill in some details about what had happened at the salvage property that fateful Monday afternoon. At most, they hoped to gather a nugget or two of incriminating evidence, later admissible in court, against Brendan's uncle Steve.

We knew Brendan spent a lot of time playing video games—that's it, not much of a profile to go on. We also knew that his feisty mother, Barb Janda, Steven's younger sister, who worked the early shift at a factory job, was not home much. Instead, she spent her free time back then with her new love interest, a cousin of her estranged husband, named Scott Tadych, who lived a few miles away.

Brendan showed up for the interview looking like he always did, in baggy pants and a loose-fitting shirt, his hair rumpled. When he sat, he slouched deeply, and when asked a question, he hesitated before answering, usually with just one or two words. He didn't seem nervous or agitated. His answers didn't seem in any way evasive—at least in the beginning of the conversation.

About ten minutes in, Brendan surprised Fassbender and Wiegert. He told them he'd seen a "dark reddish liquid" on his uncle's garage floor, as well as a bag of what he thought were Teresa's clothes. Steven Avery, Brendan said, had asked him to help clean the garage floor with bleach and paint thinner. When Brendan explained that he'd helped gather wood and tires to throw on the "big bonfire" that evening, the two investigators knew that Brendan could likely provide important details regarding the timeline of the crime and his direct observations of the fire. And when he admitted seeing "toes" and "other body parts" in the fire on October 31st, Brendan Dassey morphed from just another wayward young person on the property to the most critical witness against Steven Avery.

I wanted Brendan's statements on tape, and so, after getting permission from his mother, the detectives drove him to the Two Rivers Police Department that same afternoon. Barb Janda showed up and consented to the second interview—even though such consent is not required in Wisconsin. She also declined an invitation to sit in on the interview with her son, in which he repeated the incriminating statements he'd made earlier in the day.

After the second (taped) interview, Wiegert and Fassbender briefed Barb, who was, by that time, pacing and chain-smoking. The significance of her son's disclosures surrounding the murder of Teresa Halbach hit Janda hard—she knew that Brendan would become a major witness in the case, and that the rest of the Avery family would most likely be furious that he was cooperating with police. Steven had long preached to Barb that her kids be taught "NOT to talk to the cops," and this failure of paranoiac parenting would surely be met with his disapproval, if not something worse. She was right.

To shield Barb and her children from intimidation, officers invited the Janda family to stay at a local resort, Fox Hills, many miles away from the Avery compound in Mishicot. It seemed clear that Ma and Pa Avery cared about Steven, and Steven alone. They would sacrifice their grandkids in a heartbeat, I thought, rather than give up their freshly exonerated son to the cops.

Barb agreed to move to Fox Hills for the night.

———————————

Around the conference table at the Calumet Sheriff's Department Detective Bureau, at eight o'clock the next morning, we sifted through Brendan's various admissions. Did he really see toes in the fire? Did he really see a bag of Teresa's clothes? We weren't sure. But I was certain of one thing—he knew a hell of a lot more than he was telling about what happened that night.

I looked at Tom and Mark and said, "We need to re-interview Brendan, and it needs to be on video. We may only get one shot at this statement, and before the family talks him out of cooperating, we need to get every piece of information he has." We set a date: the next day, March 1st.

Brendan was a minor, but this was a murder investigation. Dassey attended Mishicot public schools and although he received special assistance in a few classes, he knew right from wrong, was able to distinguish between the truth and a lie, and like any other sixteen-year-old in Wisconsin, was not "entitled" to the presence of an attorney or a parent during police questioning unless he asked for one. I've never been comfortable with the idea of interviewing child witnesses without some support person present, whether an attorney or a parent. But Barb was definitely a loose cannon, and nobody could assure me that she wasn't more interested in saving her brother than her own son. Her attendance at the interview wouldn't help get to the truth, especially if Brendan was more involved than we thought, so although I understood Barb would be told of the March 1st scheduled interview, I hoped she'd choose not to attend. Brendan needed to be Mirandized, certainly, but if he felt comfortable proceeding without a lawyer, I needed him questioned.

My hope was realized. Again, given a chance to sit beside her son as he spoke to homicide investigators, Barb passed.

Fassbender and Wiegert picked up Brendan at school on the first day of March, and drove him to the Manitowoc County law enforcement center. On the way to the interview, they stopped off at his house, where Dassey handed over the first piece of physical evidence in what would be a long list of items corroborating his version of the Halloween night events—the bleach-stained jeans he wore when he helped his uncle Steven clean blood from the garage floor.

The Manitowoc County Sheriff's Department has a "soft room" for interviews, set up more like a living room than one of the drab, concrete-walled interrogation rooms seen on TV. Brendan was offered a soda and something to eat, which he declined. Around 11 AM, the interview began.

Late that afternoon, my cell phone rang.

"We need to see you," Wiegert said, urgency in his voice.

"How'd it go?"

"You aren't going to fucking believe it. Dassey confessed to raping Teresa, while Steven watched, and they killed her together."

Wiegert was right—I didn't fucking believe it.

"How did you get him to tell you all this stuff?" I asked.

"We just kept telling him, 'It's OK, Brendan, we already know what happened'—and the kid kept telling us more, and more, and more."

When I watched the tapes, all four hours of them, a few things struck me. First, Brendan spoke, or mumbled, mostly in monosyllables. Sometimes he'd make a statement, a shocking one, and then lapse into silence, rather than expanding upon it or continuing the story. It was clear that, for Brendan, providing one- or two-word answers was not a communication style limited to police interrogations. This kid probably didn't go into chapter and verse about anything in his life. Hell, he probably wasn't used to being *asked* much, by anyone, about anything.

Not only was his story halting, it contradicted itself. It was hard to separate the truths from half-truths, and impossible to tell if Brendan was still holding back. Finally, his flat affect— Brendan's failure to demonstrate any emotion when discussing raping, killing, and burning the corpse of a young woman—was unsettling. I didn't know if he was a psychopath, mentally ill, an accomplished liar, or just dumb as a post. In the end, I was certain of only two things—Brendan Dassey was there, and he helped.

On May 13th, 2006, in a videotaped interview lasting about two hours, Brendan told a slightly different story than he provided on March 1st, one I believe corresponds more closely to the architecture of what happened on the Avery property that fateful Halloween. This confession is never presented in *Making a Murderer*, none of the details so much as hinted at.

In the May 13th interview, Brendan makes chilling admissions, with reasonable specificity and almost no prompting by the investigators. He says that he went to the Steven Avery residence on two separate occasions on October 31st, first at around 4 PM, after he and brother Blaine came home from school, then again after dark, when he admits he raped the bound photographer. Dassey confirmed that Steven likely sexually assaulted the victim between the times of his visits. Avery gave Brendan some money from Teresa Halbach's purse; his uncle, Brendan said, burned the rest of the purse's contents, including the victim's digital camera and phone, in his own burn barrel—as confirmed by the recovered physical evidence.

The starkest difference between the story Brendan originally told in his March confession and the version of events he presents in May is that, in his later confession, the murder occurred in the garage, not in his uncle's bedroom. Dassey details how he and his uncle cleaned up the blood on the garage floor using Halbach's own clothing, with heavy applications of bleach and paint thinner. He admits to helping Steven carry Teresa to the big fire in the backyard, adding tires and other materials to hasten the process of evidence destruction. He describes the horrible smell of a burning body—a smell that those unfortunate enough to experience can tell you they will never forget. He witnesses Steven chopping up Teresa's bones as they burned.

Brendan also describes his relationship with his uncle, including reminders from the seasoned criminal never to talk to the cops, and troubling allegations of Uncle Steve touching his genitals. Steven also hinted, Brendan says, at his motive for Teresa's abduction, rape, and murder—Avery was pissed off that his fiancée, Jodi, was in jail, and that he hadn't "gotten any" for a while, something he discussed with Dassey on Saturday, October 29th, two days before the actual rape and murder took place. Dassey admits to helping his uncle hide the SUV down "by the pit" the evening of October 31st, and says they drove the vehicle "the back way" around the salvage yard to deposit the car. Steven had every intention of crushing the SUV, according to Brendan, but he waited too long. Pam Sturm, a citizen searcher, discovered the RAV4 on the morning of Saturday, November 5th—before he'd had a chance to crush it.

Avery seems to have gambled that the vastness of the family salvage yard, those forty eerie acres of rusting cars and trucks, would be his salvation, that he had plenty of time to get back to the car, remove the makeshift camouflage, use the retained key to drive the RAV4 over to the crusher, and eliminate, in a head-splitting squeal of metal against metal, most of the evidence that could ultimately be used against him.

Later that Saturday, having accompanied the Avery family to their cottage in Crivitz, and after learning of the SUV's discovery, Uncle Steven's first instinct was to hide from law enforcement. It was Steve's father, Allan Avery, Brendan said, who counseled Steven that "if you hide, it will look like you did it." Steve changed his bet, gambling instead that, having been wrongfully convicted once, he could convince the world it was happening again.

Steven Avery also seems to have bet that his faithful nephew would keep his mouth shut, perhaps assuming that Brendan's involvement would guarantee his silence. On both counts, he gambled wrong.

———————

Brendan Dassey provided valuable components of the State's overall case. He set forth the first narrative as to how Teresa Halbach was killed, and pointed us to physical evidence of the crime, including the bullet fragment under the air compressor in the Avery garage that harbored the DNA of Teresa Halbach. Without Brendan's statement as to *where* the murder occurred, the police would never have gotten a search warrant and found that bullet.

Brendan provided an explanation for how the victim's blood got into the rear cargo area of her Toyota RAV4. After Steven Avery shot Teresa Halbach in the garage, he and Brendan wrapped her in bedding and tossed her in the back of her own SUV while they thought about how to dispose of Teresa's body. (According to Brendan, they were originally going to dump her in the pond, but decided the water level was too low.) Soaked in blood, her head lay against the side cargo panel of the vehicle, leaving the bloody hair pattern that experts would later identify for the jury.

But that wasn't all. Brendan also told investigators that Uncle Steven reached under the Toyota RAV4 hood, which officers believed was to unhook the battery. Sergeant Bill Tyson, making damn sure to first put on fresh latex gloves, swabbed the hood latch of the SUV after it was returned to Calumet County from the crime lab in April 2006. It revealed "non-blood" DNA of the defendant, Steven Avery, to the exclusion of any other DNA in the world, most probably skin cells sloughed off of Avery's sweaty hands. Avery's DNA on the hood latch means that it was

Steven himself who reached under the victim's vehicle hood, only accessed after the hood release is triggered from inside the vehicle. Even if a cop could plant skin cells on a hood latch, why would he? How would he have known Brendan would lead us to test it months later? *Making a Murderer* excludes any mention of the hood-latch DNA.

But Brendan Dassey's confession didn't spell the end for Steven Avery. For one thing, I didn't introduce Brendan's damning statements into Steven Avery's jury trial—I was legally prohibited from calling him as a witness without a plea bargain in place. Brendan had a Fifth Amendment right against self-incrimination. If I'd called him to testify, his testimony would not just incriminate Steven Avery, it would also incriminate him. So, unless we'd cut a deal with Dassey's attorney, which we hadn't, we couldn't legally call Brendan to the stand. Let me say that again—I never used Brendan Dassey's statements, any of them, to convict Steven Avery.

Avery was convicted primarily on the forensic evidence recovered at the scene: the blood, the key, the bones, and the bullet. Steven sunk himself.

The question remained, however: Would Brendan Dassey's own statements spell the end for him? Would they send him to prison for life? Would he sink himself, and follow in the muddy footsteps of Uncle Steven?

Aerial photo of 40-acre Avery Salvage yard

Avery Salvage car crusher

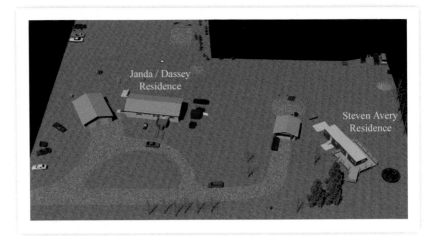

Exterior Diagram of Avery and Janda Property

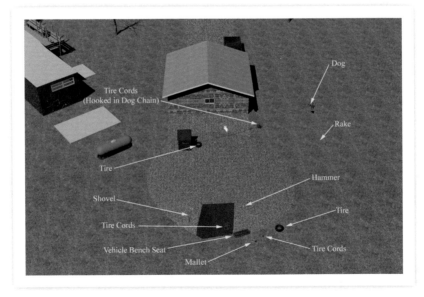

Diagram of the burn pit

Avery's dog, "Bear," guarding the burn pit

Avery's front yard, with burn barrel

Avery's burn barrel containing Teresa Halbach's electronics

Teresa's electronics recovered from Avery's burn barrel

Rivet from Daisy Fuentes jeans, recovered from burn pit

Hood latch of the RAV4, from which Avery's DNA was recovered

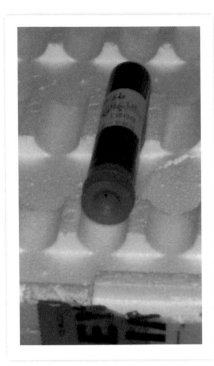

Blood vial located in clerk of court's file

Blood smear near ignition of RAV4

Bloodstain on back door

Bloodstained cargo area of Halbach SUV (rubber mat missing)

Teresa Halbach's SUV, found covered with branches and debris

License plate
from RAV4,
recovered, folded,
found inside of
another junked
vehicle

Teresa's key found in Avery bedroom, fallen from behind bookcase

Teresa's key (from Avery's bedroom) with lanyard (from RAV4)

Teresa's key with blue fob

Leg bone, with tissue identified as belonging to Teresa Halbach

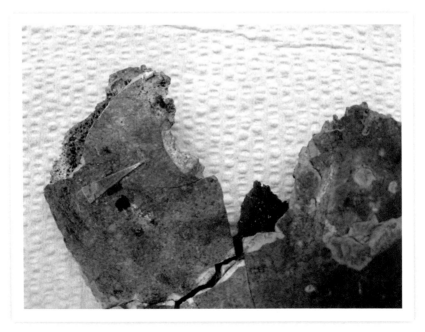

Skull fragment showing beveling from bullet wound

Avery's garage in November (bullet recovered in March, 2006, from under green air compressor in back)

.22 cal rifle recovered from Steven Avery's bedroom, from which bullet recovered with Halbach's DNA was fired

Bones recovered from Avery burn pit

Bone fragments entwined in steel belts from tires

Andy Colborn

Jim Lenk

The prosecution team in the "war room"
(Tom Fallon, Ken Kratz, Norm Gahn)

Tom Fassbender

Endangered Missing

Teresa Halbach

Birth:	3/22/1980	Hair:	Lt Brown
Missing:	10/3105	Eyes:	Brown
Race:	White	Height:	5'6"
Sex:	Female	Weight:	135#

Missing From: Manitowoc/Two Rivers, WI
Age Missing: 25   Age Now 25

Teresa Halbach was last seen on Monday, October 31, 2005 in the Manitowoc/Two Rivers area, but may have been traveled further to Green Bay or the Fox Cities. She was driving a 1999 dark green Toyota Rav 4, license plate number SWH582. She was wearing blue jeans, white button-down shirt, and a spring jacket.

IF YOU HAVE ANY INFORMATION PLEASE CONTACT
Calumet County Sheriff's Department, (920) 849-2335 or
Youth Educated in Safety, Inc. 1-800-272-7715

GUARDIAN

Teresa Halbach's Missing Person poster

Teresa with her RAV4

Teresa Halbach, 3/22/80–10/31/05

CHAPTER TEN

The Decision

Ten years after Brendan Dassey confessed to Teresa Halbach's rape, murder, and mutilation, his legal team convinced a federal district court magistrate that not only had every one of the Wisconsin state courts to review Dassey's case in the years after his conviction ruled incorrectly, but also that *no court*—not one, in all the land—could reasonably have concluded that Brendan's statement given on March 1st, 2006, was voluntary. Put simply, US Magistrate Judge William E. Duffin held that the Wisconsin courts were not just wrong, they were "unreasonable," and Brendan should be sent home.

The ninety-one-page opinion cited cases undermining its own conclusions, and seemed, to me, determined to spring Dassey—logic and applicable case law be damned. It also turned aside reasoned decisions by three State of Wisconsin courts.

This ruling was the most dramatic development in the Avery/ Dassey case since *Making a Murderer* debuted almost a year earlier, in December of 2015. It set up the possibility that Brendan would walk out of the Columbia Correctional Institution in Portage, Wisconsin, where he is currently housed. (For security reasons, he had been transferred from Green Bay Correctional—forty miles from Manitowoc County—the same prison where Steven Avery served much of the eighteen years he spent behind bars for the sexual assault of Penny Beernsten before DNA evidence set him free.)

So let's delve into The Big Decision. Duffin ruled that the March 1st confession was involuntary because Brendan was a juvenile, had an IQ in the low seventies, spoke to Wiegert and Fassbender without an attorney or a parent present, and was repeatedly told by the cops that they "already knew what happened" and "it will be OK." Duffin admits that none of these factors alone, or even several in combination, were enough to render the statement involuntary—the existing case law is quite clear on that. Yet somehow he, alone of the judges who have ruled on the matter, saw that this "totality of circumstances" required that Dassey's convictions be overturned.

Before Brendan Dassey went to trial, a suppression hearing was held to determine whether his statements to the two detectives would be admitted into evidence. The standard for admissibility of statements taken from teenagers is the same as the standard for adults: the statements must have been voluntarily given, free of threats or promises by interrogators. It's the same admissibility standard followed in every state, not just Wisconsin.

Brendan's defense team argued that his intellectual limitations made him unusually susceptible to police interrogation tactics. In other words, they argued that he was not *able* to resist the suggestions of the interrogating officers, and that he just told them what they wanted to hear, without appreciation for the trouble he was getting himself into. If this was determined to be true, Brendan's statements would be deemed "involuntary" and excluded by the court, crippling the Dassey murder and rape prosecution.

After reviewing all of Dassey's statements to law enforcement, Judge Jerome Fox of the Manitowoc County Circuit Court ruled that Brendan voluntarily provided answers to questions, free from any coercion or undue influence. Specifically, the judge found:

> *He [Dassey] displayed no difficulty in understanding the questions asked of him. At no time did he ask to stop the interview or request that his mother or a lawyer be present. Instead, he answered the questions put to him. Sometimes he revised his answers after being prodded to be truthful or being told by his questioners that they knew his answer was either incomplete or untrue and he should be honest. These appeals to honesty made by the interviewers were nothing more than a reminder to Brendan Dassey that he had a moral duty to tell the truth.*

On thirteen specific occasions in the March 1st interview alone, Brendan resisted suggestion by interrogators. How many of those thirteen moments appear in *Making a Murderer? Zero.* The audience sees only moments when Brendan appears to adopt what the cops say.

Dassey not only resisted suggestions by Fassbender and Wiegert, but corrected them when they mischaracterized what he said. As an example, when Wiegert wondered if Brendan fired the gun at Teresa, he replied, "No—I could never shoot her," and recounted a time when he was younger, when "he could not even shoot a cat," implying that he was uncomfortable around guns being discharged at living beings. He said he had to turn away when his uncle shot Teresa in the head. When Brendan described Teresa's body, investigators said they "knew" Teresa had a tattoo on her stomach (she did not) to see if Brendan would then "remember" seeing it. He did not. Multiple times, Brendan Dassey told the cops, "I didn't do that" or "It didn't happen that way."

Dassey's defense team lost their suppression hearing arguments in the circuit court, they lost a post-conviction motion for a new trial on similar grounds, and they also failed in the Wisconsin Court of Appeals, where their coercion argument was rejected yet again. The Wisconsin Supreme Court declined to even hear the case.

———————

Those numerous times when Brendan resisted suggestion by interrogators, never shown in *Making a Murderer*, are likewise absent from Magistrate Duffin's decision. Instead, he cites the twenty-four times that investigators told Brendan that they "already knew what happened," and implored him to tell the truth.

Duffin notes that Investigator Wiegert told Dassey that he couldn't make any promises, but in the same paragraph, the magistrate claims that this was "drowned out" by police assurances that Dassey had nothing to worry about. The opinion concedes that there was "no single statement by the investigators [which] rendered Dassey's statement involuntary," and that the officers used "calm tones" and "never used aggressive or confrontational tactics." Nevertheless, the magistrate held that the interrogators' statements that they already knew everything and that Brendan would "be OK" collectively resulted in "impermissible promises" made to the sixteen-year-old suspect.

If officers had said just one or the other, Duffin reasoned, the statement would be admissible: it was only the combination that implied to Dassey that the officers knew the full extent of his crimes and that he would not be harshly punished for them.

The magistrate construes this as a case where two *permissible* questioning tactics combined to create a constitutionally impermissible impression—an impression the intellectually limited Dassey allegedly would have picked up on, despite the fact that, according to Duffin, the officers themselves may very well have been unaware that the combination created this impression.

Rather than an intentional and concerted effort to trick Dassey into confessing, what occurred here may have been the product of the investigators failing to appreciate how combining statements that they already "knew everything that happened" with assurances that Dassey was "OK" and had

nothing to worry about collectively resulted in constitution-
ally impermissible promises.

I've made it a practice not to publicly criticize or second-guess judges, or discuss their possible motives for decisions they have rendered, but how on earth does that make sense? Talk about "unreasonable"! Dassey is too stupid to realize he is incriminating himself in a murder, but savvy enough to appreciate that the combination of "we already know" and "you will be OK" means that he won't be charged with murder as a result? Furthermore, in his own opinion, Duffin points to case law in which "reasonable" courts ruled just as the Wisconsin Court of Appeals did, undermining his stated claim that Dassey met the "no reasonable court" standard. He made the state's argument for them—it's *Duffin v. Duffin!*

The federal district court gave the State of Wisconsin three options: (1) release Dassey within ninety days; (2) appeal the court's decision to the federal district court of appeals; or (3) retry Dassey without using the March 1st statement.

In September of 2016, Wisconsin Attorney General Brad Schimel selected the second option. The Department of Justice appealed Magistrate Duffin's decision to the United States Seventh Circuit Court of Appeals. Said Schimel:

We believe the magistrate judge's decision that Brendan Dassey's confession was coerced by investigators, and that no reasonable court could have concluded otherwise, is wrong on the facts and wrong on the law. Two state courts carefully examined the evidence and properly concluded that Brendan Dassey's confession to sexually assaulting and murdering Teresa Halbach with his uncle, Steven Avery, was voluntary, and the investigators did not use constitutionally impermissible tactics.

———————

The Duffin ruling infuriated former DCI agent Tom Fassender. Before the critical March 1st interview, Tom felt bad for Brendan, who was clearly upset by whatever had happened on Halloween with his uncle Steven. When Tom acted, as the magistrate put it, "parental," he wasn't acting. He was being genuine. And he was honestly indicating that from what he had seen and heard *up to that point*, he thought Dassey would be "OK," that he'd never graduate from witness to suspect. At that point, Tom thought that even if Brendan told everything he knew, he would only further implicate Steven in the crimes.

Tom's retired now. But he hasn't forgotten.

"I was a law enforcement officer for over thirty years and was a good, ethical cop who followed the law and rules," he says. "I've always followed the rules of investigation and interrogation and even taught recruits, officers, and investigators on those topics. My career track record bears that out. If anything, during my career, I was often taken advantage of during interviews because I wanted to give the subject the benefit of the doubt if possible and always felt empathy for the subject. I did not deviate from these principles during this investigation. I guarantee, if anything illegal or unethical had occurred on the Halbach investigation, I would have been the first to sound the alarm. Those were good cops and people that worked on that case."

That's the Tom Fassbender I know and respect, the man whose reputation is under attack yet again, all these years later.

This may surprise you, but there is one opinion I share with even the most rabid factions of the *Making a Murderer* audience, and that is that Brendan ended up a sort of sacrificial lamb. We may disagree on who is responsible for this, but make no mistake—Brendan is a victim in his own way, and I have a lot of sympathy for him. I've said that for years.

There is almost universal belief, among law enforcement, prosecution, defense, and court officials, that Brendan Dassey was no murderer. He was a sixteen-year-old kid who played video games and idolized his uncle Steve. Left to his own devices, he never would have raped or murdered Teresa Halbach. But he became a murderer—and it was Steven Avery who made him one.

Whatever you believe about which specific acts he committed that night, Brendan Dassey was involved. As I told the jury at his trial, he was there—and he helped. When he recanted his confession so completely, insisting in the end that he had not even seen evidence of the crime, which was an obvious lie, he left the prosecution with few options. He was offered a very fair plea agreement—serving as little as fifteen years for his role in the crimes in exchange for truthful testimony against his uncle. He could very well have enjoyed the majority of his adult life as a free man. And yet, it was his own family who pressured Dassey to turn down the deal. Why?

Because while a plea agreement would have dramatically benefited Brendan, it would have just as dramatically hurt Steven Avery's chances of acquittal. The "planting" defense advanced by Strang and Buting wouldn't carry much weight with a jury who hears the defendant's own nephew testify that he witnessed Steven kill Teresa and mutilate and dispose of her body.

Steven's defense, I believe, trumped all else.

His high-profile exoneration and the civil lawsuit that followed brought both local celebrity and the promise of a significant windfall, money that was expected to flow in the direction of the Avery salvage yard. In a phone call on May 22nd, 2006, Steven Avery tells Brendan's mom, Barb Janda, "Brendan can't take the plea bargain." But who could convince Brendan that only serving fifteen years for rape and murder was a bad deal for him?

Enter Allan Avery.

In early June 2006, Brendan Dassey was informed that the family patriarch, Steven's father and Brendan's grandfather, usually not much given to phone calls with his incarcerated kin, wanted to "talk" to Brendan. A clearly concerned Brendan Dassey asks his grandmother, mother, and Aunt Candy why his grandfather wants to speak to him—nobody provides a hint to the teen inmate, other than to reiterate *Grandpa needs to talk to you.*

On June 6th, 2006, Allan Avery speaks to Brendan Dassey. It's the only jail call recorded between Dassey and his grandfather, and therefore the significance and weight Brendan gives to the call is obvious. Allan reminds Brendan to avoid talking with the police, as they are "bastards" and can't be trusted. "Stick to your guns," he tells Brendan, and "don't go for a plea bargain." Allan Avery says that the State wants to send Dassey to prison for life—"Listen to your grandpa," he says. Then, tipping his hand as to whom the "no plea bargain" strategy will actually benefit, Allan tells Brendan that taking a plea bargain will only "hurt both of you guys" [Dassey and Steven].

Brendan Dassey complies. Dassey's new lawyers decide to go to trial, and have not been shy about disclosing that *Dassey's family* would not allow him to accept a plea bargain. Brendan is convicted, of course, and sentenced to life in prison. The lamb was laid down. His uncle made him a murderer. His family helped send him to prison, and sadly, depending on the federal appeals court, may have tossed away the key.

I often wonder how Brendan feels now about the advice furnished by his loved ones. Brendan will likely benefit in some degree from the federal ruling suppressing his March 1st confession (Magistrate Duffin ordered Brendan's release on bond pending appeal, an extraordinary ruling given Dassey was convicted of rape and murder by a jury—the 7th Circuit Court of Appeals rejected that effort on November 17, 2016, and ordered Dassey remain in prison while the appeal progresses). Still, he will have lost many years of his young adult life as a result of being talked, by members of his own family, into decisions that were not in his best interest. Decisions only furthering the interests of one man—Steven Avery.

I have one major regret in my prosecution of the Halbach case, and that is the press conference I gave on March 2nd, revealing some of the graphic details contained in Dassey's criminal complaint. *Making a Murderer* seems to imply I loved and often courted the media, which wasn't the case at all. Other than that on March 2nd, I gave only one other short press conference during the eighteen months the case was pending in court. Fifteen months elapsed between charging Steven Avery and going to trial—and I spoke twice to the media during that time. Believe it or not, I was frustrated with the media frenzy surrounding the case, and was certainly not trying to add to it. The Avery case was not just a matter of general public interest, it had become a full-blown media circus, and over the previous month, the defense team had taken several opportunities to publicly trumpet their defense: that Steven Avery, local celebrity and poster child for The Innocence Project, was the victim of police misconduct and framing.

The rules of attorney professional conduct allowed me to make whatever public statements were necessary to "cure" the defense attempts to prejudice the potential jury pool. Given that, I hoped speaking about the details of the Dassey complaint would counter the "poor Steven" narrative advanced by Strang and Buting—and, ironically, I also hoped it would be enough to prevent the media from sharing even further salacious specifics.

In retrospect, I wish I had simply released the Dassey charging document and said nothing at all. The result would have been the

same, given the media climate of the case, except it would not have
been my face telling the story. It would have been the better choice.

But I lose no sleep over my prosecution of Brendan Dassey. I
was a prosecutor with a dead young woman and her surviving family for which to pursue justice. It was not my fault that Brendan
was easily manipulated by Avery, or had a low IQ, or was shy, or
that he made a dozen inconsistent statements. I believe Brendan
could have saved Teresa's life, but chose instead to involve himself
in the rape, murder, and mutilation of an innocent woman. I have
always said that he did not deserve life in prison, and should have
taken the plea bargain that I offered him. But I couldn't, and can't,
make Brendan's choices for him.

As I mentioned before, the US Seventh Circuit Court of
Appeals, comprising a more "seasoned" panel of appellate judges,
will review the "voluntariness" issue, taking it out of the hands of
what appears to me to be a magistrate at the district court level.
There is a larger issue at stake if this decision is allowed to stand,
after all—it flies in the face of other case law and, without clarification, is sure to cause confusion for law enforcement and the courts
about both the standards for voluntary confessions and the standards for granting federal *habeas* relief. My prediction, for what it's
worth, is that the Seventh Circuit will overturn Magistrate Duffin's
decision, finding that the interrogation of Brendan Dassey was voluntary, free of any coercion or promises having been made.

If the State of Wisconsin loses that appeal, and Brendan shuffles out of prison, I wonder how he will have changed, what the
rest of his life will be like. Will history repeat itself in Manitowoc

County? How long will it be before a second member of the Avery clan shows up in civil court to file a multimillion-dollar lawsuit alleging wrongful conviction or police misconduct? Will he follow Uncle Steven's lead again? Where will he place the blame for his misfortune; will he take the life of another in retaliation? If he does, I'm certain the *Making a Murderer* cameras will return to Wisconsin to capture the aftermath.

CHAPTER ELEVEN

The Villains

Imagine signing up for a lifetime of bringing those who harm others to justice, and then being accused, wrongly, of conspiring to frame an innocent man for murder, and maybe even killing a young woman. Imagine living with these accusations, for which no proof is ever offered, for a quarter of your life. Imagine patrolling snowy Midwestern back roads, faithfully, anonymously, for decades, and then being featured as a bad guy in a television show seen by millions around the world, a show deemed worthy of Hollywood's highest honors. Let's look at two officers who suffered this fate. They won't win an Emmy for the performance of their duties, but that's OK with them.

Andy and Jim.

Andy is the model Midwestern cop: up through the ranks, a record as unblemished as his uniform; but also a man with a common touch, a cop who was born in, lives in, and will always live in the community he protects—the kind of cop rural Wisconsin cherishes. Soft-spoken, a man who looks you straight in the eye and always means what he says—that's Andy. Sappy, right? Perhaps from a big-city perspective. Not to us Cheeseheads.

In 1995, seven years removed from a decade-long tour of duty in the US Air Force, Andy Colborn, then thirty-five, worked for the Manitowoc County Sheriff's Department as a corrections officer. One day, he fielded a call from another law enforcement agency: they had a guy in lockup bragging about assaulting some lady in Manitowoc County, claiming another guy got arrested for it and sent to prison. This meant nothing to Andy, who transferred the call to the detective unit.

Done. Finished. Kaput. That was the full extent of Andy's connection to Steven Avery's sexual assault case, the one that would see Avery exonerated after serving eighteen years in state prison. Andy knew the Avery family well; he bought car parts from them. "I didn't care if Steve got $100 billion from his lawsuit against Manitowoc County. Not a dime of that was coming out of my pocket. The man deserved to get paid."

Hell, even the Avery family grew its share of cops. Manitowoc deputy Arland Avery, the brother of Steven Avery's father, Allan, helped train Andy Colborn as a young officer. So, when Teresa Halbach disappeared, and then her RAV4 was found on the Avery salvage yard, "I didn't think Steven would be dumb enough to be involved in something like this when things were going so well for him," Andy says. "Why would he throw that all away, when his payday was coming? Steven had turned his life around. He could have bought himself an island and gotten away from all this."

———————

On November 3rd, 2005, Andy took a call that would nearly derail his career and infect one of the most even-tempered men I know with an anger and bitterness he should never have had to suffer. It was Calumet County Sheriff's Investigator Mark Wiegert on the line. Teresa Halbach had been reported missing.

In a recorded call, not played in the Netflix docuseries, Wiegert tells Colborn the make, model, and plate number of Teresa's SUV. Immediately thereafter, as is customary, Colborn calls dispatch to verify the plate.

At trial, defense attorneys suggested that Colborn found Teresa's car on November 3rd, and then called dispatch, reading off the plate number to confirm that it was hers. The not-so-subtle implication, of course, was that Sgt. Andy Colborn was responsible for, or at least complicit in, the framing of Steven Avery. Dean Strang cross-examined Sergeant Colborn about his call from Wiegert and subsequent call to dispatch, and this exchange appeared at the end of Episode 5 of *Making a Murderer*. Well, sort of.

In one of the more shocking bits of editing in the series, the back-and-forth between Strang and Andy Colborn is spliced together so that Colborn is shown answering "Yes" to a question that he never actually answered in court. Colborn's "Yes" was spliced into the show from a different part of his testimony. The filmmakers omit a question about the routine nature of the license check, and replace it with a fabricated exchange that has Sergeant Colborn agreeing that his call might be viewed as suspicious.

See for yourself. Below on the left is an excerpt from *Making a Murderer*, Episode 5. On the right is a transcript of Colborn's testimony on Day 7 of the Avery trial. For the jury, Strang has just played Colborn's call to dispatch, in which he gives the dispatcher Halbach's plate number. Strang asks Colborn whether Wiegert gave him the number.

Here's what follows:

Making a Murderer, Episode 5	Trial Transcript
Colborn: He had to have given it to me, because I wouldn't have had the number any other way.	**Colborn**: He had to have given it to me, because I wouldn't have had the number any other way.
Strang: Well, you can understand how someone listening to that might think that you were calling in a license plate that you were looking at on the back end of a 1999 Toyota.	**Strang**: Well, and you can understand how someone listening to that might think that you were calling in a license plate that you were looking at on the back end of a 1999 Toyota; from listening to that tape, you can understand why someone might think that, can't you?
Colborn: **Yes.**	**Attorney Kratz**: **It's a conclusion, Judge. He's conveying the problems to the jury.**

Strang: But there's no way you should have been looking at Teresa Halbach's license plate on November three, on the back end of a 1999 Toyota?

Colborn: I shouldn't have been and I was not looking at the license plate.

(Theme music plays)

The Court: I agree, the objection is sustained.

Strang: This call sounded like hundreds of other license plate or registration checks you have done through dispatch before?

Colborn: Yes.

Strang: But there's no way you should have been looking at Teresa Halbach's license plate on November three, on the back end of a 1999 Toyota?

Attorney Kratz: Asked and answered, Your Honor; he already said he didn't and was not looking at the license plate.

The Court: Sustained.

Strang: There's no way you should have been, is there?

Colborn: I shouldn't have been and I was not looking at the license plate.

After *Making a Murderer* came the deluge. Hundreds of calls, at home and at work, threatening Andy and his family with violence.

The phone rang for the first time on Christmas Eve, less than one week after the series was released. "I got a call from some guy in Florida who said, 'Steven Avery is right up there with some of the best people who've ever walked the face of the earth, and you should do your kids a favor and shoot yourself. If you don't, I'll come to Wisconsin and do it for you.' The guy turned out to be a five-time convicted felon." Similar calls came from Denmark, Germany, Australia, and countries around the world.

"These people have my home phone number, which is unlisted, and they know my address," says Andy. "One guy said, 'Colborn, you're headed to prison, where you won't last two days. Or you'll be killed when you get out. And I'll see to it that friends of mine gang-rape your wife.'"

But this was only the latest example of the public abuse Andy—and his family—have endured. *Making a Murderer* came out in 2015; the accusations had first been made a decade earlier.

"One day, after the defense first accused me of being dishonest, my sixth-grade son was getting on the school bus when reporters approached him, asking what he thought about his dad being called a crook," Andy says. When the principal asked reporters to leave the boy alone, they retorted that it was a public school and they could be there whenever they wanted.

After *Making a Murderer*, Andy received enough serious and credible threats that the FBI was asked to investigate. "My wife, Barb, is legally blind," says Colborn, now supervisor of the detective unit at the sheriff's department. "Because she's afraid to be home alone, I bought her a gun." And though he's still a cop, Andy, who has two sons in the military, says, "I no longer encourage my boys to pursue law enforcement careers."

Andy has trouble sleeping. "I can't fall asleep before two AM, and I'm usually up by four thirty. All I can think about is that somebody's going to show up and harm my family when I'm at work."

But off to work he goes, every day. "The reputation of a law enforcement officer has to be above reproach," says Andy Colborn. "You can't succeed in this career if you're a liar. I spent my entire career building my reputation. I'm not about to lose my job because of Steven Avery. I can't help that he hid Teresa Halbach's key in his bedroom, or that I was there when it was found."

Meet Villain Number Two: Andy's colleague, Lieutenant James Lenk, a former Detroit cop who joined the Manitowoc Sheriff's Department in 1988, and by 2005 headed the detective unit. An avid camper, Jim adjusted to Wisconsin quickly, and he and his wife, a former nurse, became fixtures of their church community. Slender and bespectacled, Jim looks more like a professor than some hard-boiled police detective, but his smart and careful detective work earned him commendations from his superiors and the respect of his peers and community alike.

In his closing argument, Jerry Buting pointed out that Manitowoc County sheriff's deputies, including Lt. Jim Lenk, had 24/7 access to the Manitowoc County Clerk of Courts Office, where Steven Avery's blood vial had been housed for more than a decade. However, in a recent conversation with me, Lenk emphasized that not only was he unaware of the existence of the Avery blood vial in the clerk of court's office in 2002, he "never even knew the blood vial existed anywhere."

For twenty years, Jim Lenk oversaw the evidence room for the sheriff's department. As the property officer, Lenk explained, "I would often be the one to sign for evidence when it went out [to the crime lab], or when it was sent back after testing." But given that the vial was neither requested nor sent with the other evidence in 2002, the suggestion that Lieutenant Lenk signed for its transmission to the crime lab is simply untrue.

Jim Lenk was living in Michigan when the Beernsten case was being prosecuted in 1985—he had no involvement in the case that sent Steven Avery to prison. And in 1995, when Andy Colborn transferred that call claiming Manitowoc may have imprisoned the wrong guy for an assault, Lenk was *not* the detective who received the call, as is commonly thought. When Sergeant Colborn heard about Avery's exoneration in 2003, and decided to mention the call from eight years earlier in case it might somehow be related, Lieutenant Lenk talked to Sheriff Ken Petersen about the call, and had no further involvement. It was enough to get him deposed, like many other Manitowoc County employees, in Avery's civil lawsuit, but he had no actual connection to the Avery exoneration case.

I asked Jim Lenk why he volunteered to help Calumet County and DCI on November 5th, just three weeks after being deposed, and Jim explained, "I was a trained evidence tech, the one resource they badly needed on the fifth. Andy, Dave Remiker, and I were the sheriff's employees who had been the least involved in any of the Steven Avery cases, and Remiker volunteered the three of us. It was because we were *not* involved with Avery that we participated in the searches."

The defense team's accusations of evidence tampering began in February of 2006, and by the time of the trial a year later, Lenk's picture would be plastered across newspapers, with captions reading "Police Corruption Alleged." Angry as he was then, Jim never said a word in public.

"The attorneys had no evidence, but needed to blame someone," Jim says now. "For the first time in my life, I thought 'I don't need to be in this profession if this is going to be how I'm treated.'"

Colleagues in the sheriff's department joked that the Avery defense lawyers couldn't have picked two worse guys to accuse of dishonesty, as they'd chosen the two straightest arrows in the department. Everyone knew Jim and Andy as 100 percent honest. Lenk retired in 2011.

Now, Jim and his wife Marla live in a retirement community in Arizona. "Like everybody else who was involved, as soon as this thing came out, our sense of safety and peace was gone. Reporters followed us around town, sticking microphones in our faces, so bad that we had to seek refuge at the local police station," Lenk recalls. "Death threats, nasty comments from strangers in restaurants . . . It's unbelievable that I am now known for being a crooked cop."

But it isn't the loss of his reputation that bothers him the most; it's the effect it's had on his health. Eight days after *Making a Murderer* was released, James Lenk suffered a serious heart attack, directly attributed to the stress and emotional upheaval of being accused of corruption and dishonesty, all over again.

"All I ever wanted, my entire career, was to be known as an honest cop. It felt like I was punched in the stomach the first time these [defense] attorneys accused me and Andy of planting evidence. Actually, I thought he [Avery] was entitled to compensation for being wrongly convicted and imprisoned for all those years. Not only was I not upset that he sued the county, I thought he deserved to be paid."

Steven Avery may have deserved to be paid for the injustice visited upon him in 1985, but surely Andy Colborn and Jim Lenk deserve none of what they've suffered in the wake of Avery's arrest and, later, the release of *Making a Murderer*. What compensation are they entitled to?

To date, neither Andy nor Jim has watched the Netflix series, nor do they intend to.

CHAPTER TWELVE

The "Prize"

Why did I do it?

Thirty times!

Why did I send sexually suggestive text messages, thirty over the course of three days, to a crime victim who needed my help? Why did I risk throwing my career away to date a young woman who'd been knocked around by her ex-boyfriend and was in a completely vulnerable position?

Thirty times!

Many *Making a Murderer* viewers thought the answer simple—horny guy in position of power using that position to hook up. To me, the explanation was a bit more nuanced. Prescription drugs shaved away my inhibitions, and I had an untreated sexual addiction. I was a narcissist—whether it sprung from childhood or my working life, some quirk of my psyche demanded I be in control at all times, the center of attention.

And, never, ever could I be wrong. And so, believing I wasn't committing a crime or an ethics violation, I thought I could get away with the flirtation. And I almost did.

Let's go back to October 20th of 2009, when it all began, a typical fifty-one-degree October day in rural Wisconsin. The Avery case had wrapped up two and a half years earlier. Handling the usual sexual assault, drug, and property crime cases, I'd become bored. I didn't want to be a prosecutor forever. Private practice, teaching, becoming a judge, running for attorney general or Congress: all seemed viable options.

Personally, I was far less squared away.

After eighteen months in the nationwide spotlight with the Avery and Dassey prosecution, I suffered the hangover that comes when that spotlight goes dark. I'd left my five-piece classic rock band (which then included current Wisconsin Attorney General Brad Schimel, on bass). My new hobbies, tennis and tournament poker, didn't thrill me in the same way as being onstage had—figuratively with the Avery/Dassey jury trials and literally with my bandmates.

In my thirst for excitement, I'd become a serial cheater, relishing the secrecy and the risk, and eventually torpedoing my marriage.

That very day, I'd separated from my wife of ten years, and arranged to move into a friend's apartment in Appleton.

Also, on October 20th, 2009, a tall, attractive young woman named Stephanie Van Groll walked into the district attorney's office in Chilton. After an alcohol-fueled fight in a parking lot,

Stephanie's ex-boyfriend had been charged with beating and choking her, leaving scratches and bruises.

By that day, those injuries had faded.

We discussed the charges against her ex, and then the conversation turned personal. Single at the time, Stephanie tended bar and wanted to be a ranger in the Wisconsin park system. Somehow, from the way she sat and talked, I got the impression that she was coming on to me.

Wrong.

I had been using a combination of Ambien, Vicodin, and Xanax, not exactly conducive to clear thinking. After the fifteen-minute meeting, Stephanie gave me her cell phone number, in case there were updates about the case. I popped another Vicodin.

Doctors had prescribed these medications—the Xanax for my anxiety, the Ambien for sleep, and the Vicodin for pain associated with a prior surgery—and I had a few leftovers lying around. Seemed as good a time as any to finish them up.

Feeling no inhibitions that afternoon, I texted Stephanie.

"I wish you weren't one of this office's clients," I wrote from my desk, using my private phone. "You'd be a cool person to know."

Awkwardly and aggressively, the next day I upped the ante, sending nineteen more text messages. One read, "Are you the kind of girl that likes secret contact with an older married elected DA . . . the riskier the better?"

"You're pretty," I told Stephanie on the third day, October 22nd. And then I typed the sentences that made me a laughingstock not just in Wisconsin, but around the world: "I'm the atty. I have the $350,000 house. I have the 6 figure career. You may be the tall, young, hot nymph, but I am the prize!" I added that "I would not expect you to be the other woman. I would want you to be so hot and treat me so well that you'd be THE woman. R U that good?"

You want to pick two hours of your life to relive? I'd pick that afternoon, when I believed, after all the media attention the Avery trial had brought me, after convicting one of Wisconsin's most notorious killers, that I could impress a young woman with my house and income, neither of which were that impressive—especially considering they were connected to a fifty-year-old, rotund, squeaky-voiced creeper.

Stephanie responded to a few of my texts, but only with a single word or a couple of words. There was nothing in those words I should have interpreted as encouragement, and yet somehow, stupidly, I did.

Finally, I asked if she wanted to "go get a beer after this case concluded."

No response.

Struck out, I thought. Total whiff. No harm done.

Wrong again.

Accompanied by her mother, Stephanie filed a complaint against me with the Kaukauna Police Department, in the nearby county where she lived. Then Roy Korte called me. Roy headed the Criminal Litigation Unit of the Wisconsin Department of

Justice, in Madison, a division that prosecutes cases local DAs either find too complex or have conflicts with. Roy's tone of voice worried me.

"Ken," he said, "I have a complaint here against you, filed by a crime victim, and we need to talk."

I knew I'd fucked up.

The DOJ's Department of Criminal Investigation had been asked to look into Stephanie's complaint, as the Kaukauna Police Department felt they worked too closely with me to be viewed as impartial. The irony was that the DCI had been one of the lead investigative agencies in the Avery case. Roy and I agreed that a special prosecutor should be brought in to see the assault case against Stephanie's ex-boyfriend to a resolution, and that I would step aside.

As for the texting, I was mortified. But I didn't think I'd broken the law.

To commit a crime of misconduct in public office, you have to receive "something of value," for yourself or another. Asking for a date, I thought, didn't qualify.

Having justified my behavior as noncriminal, I convinced myself that no professional ethics violations had likely occurred either. I reasoned that although it is unethical in Wisconsin for an attorney to have sex with a client, Stephanie was not my "client," as the State of Wisconsin is the only client of an elected district attorney, and, anyway, I never had sex with her—the difference between sending an electronic message and "having sex" was surely clear to anyone.

The DOJ found no evidence of a crime, but that didn't end things. They called again a few weeks later and suggested that I self-report what I had done to the Office of Lawyer Regulation, the branch of the Wisconsin Supreme Court that investigates complaints against attorneys. Higher-ups at DOJ, including the AG himself, also wanted me to resign as chairman of the Wisconsin Crime Victims Right Board, a post I'd held since 1999.

Naturally, I took these developments very seriously—and very personally. I was pissed that the DOJ, which had relied on me so heavily in the Avery and Dassey cases, would put my career as district attorney in jeopardy. The DOJ, I told fellow prosecutors, ought to be thanking me for my work on the Avery case. Remember what I said about being a narcissist?

In the end, I gave in, self-reported the texting incident to the Office of Lawyer Regulation, and the next day resigned as chairman of the victims rights board. I started individual therapy. I recognized that I had a personality problem and had made some horrible life choices, but honestly, I still felt I was being singled out, perhaps to be made an example of. Mostly, I was desperate to put out this firestorm before it hit the newspapers and further consumed me.

And I didn't say a word about any of this to my estranged wife. Like the rest of the world, she wouldn't find out what had happened between me and Stephanie Van Groll until ten months later, on September 15th, 2010, when the proverbial shit really hit the fan.

The Office of Lawyer Regulation receives more than 2,000 complaints each year regarding Wisconsin attorneys. If it is determined that no ethical rule has been violated, the complaint is dismissed. I took some solace in the fact that after the Stephanie Van Groll complaint was dismissed on March 5th, 2010, she chose not to appeal the decision. I felt the ugly incident was finally behind me, secure in the knowledge that the facts giving rise to the OLR complaint would remain confidential.

The reason for keeping these dismissed matters outside public scrutiny is obvious. If an attorney is found *not* to have violated any ethical rules, he or she should be able to move forward with an untarnished professional reputation. All states have similar processes in place for dealing with complaints against lawyers, doctors, psychologists, and other licensed professions. By 2010, in Wisconsin alone, tens of thousands of lawyer grievances had been considered by the OLR since their inception. None of them—zero—had ever been reopened and/or reconsidered after being investigated and dismissed. Mine would be the first. But, before that happened, my texting scandal hit the front page.

On September 15th, 2010, a young reporter with the Associated Press, Ryan Foley, sauntered into my office in Chilton.

"I've got the text messages," said Foley, who'd worked for the AP for six years, primarily covering Wisconsin politics.

I didn't have to ask what he meant.

"This is a non-news story," I said, trying to head things off.

"Don't you think those texts are inappropriate?"

"I'm not going to comment on that."

Foley brought up his camera.

————————

In the first forty-eight hours after the AP bombshell, the shameful details found their way onto the front page of every major newspaper in Wisconsin. During the five weeks that followed, media coverage of my texting, along with new reports of various women coming forward to complain of my behavior, dominated the state and local news, and the sordid tale was covered in newspapers and on television nationally.

My hometown paper, the Appleton *Post-Crescent*, ran daily front-page stories recounting every juicy aspect of the scandal, including articles about my sexual history and personal relationships—some true, some not, but all very embarrassing. It wasn't just me, of course, who suffered the embarrassment and shame of public scrutiny. My estranged wife had microphones stuck in her face everywhere she went in town. One news crew, trying to get a comment, broke into our house, setting off the alarm. Every one of our neighbors was questioned about what they knew of my private sexual behavior. Nobody escaped the circus, not even my son, Andy, who was away at college in Whitewater, Wisconsin. I had the spotlight back, but this time I would have done anything to get rid of it.

I'd been a member of the Wisconsin District Attorneys Association since 1987, and served as its president in 1996. Two days after the scandal broke, on Friday, the WDAA sent me a letter that pulled no punches:

Your behavior involving a crime victim was repugnant and cannot be countenanced. . . . Your behavior was neither unintentional nor innocent. As a co-founder of our current victim rights system, and as a frequent lecturer on these topics, no prosecutor could be expected to know these issues better.

It was brutal to read, but it was also true.

I had coauthored much of our state's victims' rights legislation. It had been my personal cause. And now I had embarrassed myself beyond any repairable level, undermining everything I'd worked so hard to achieve. I'd turned into someone I didn't even recognize.

———————————

Cliché or not, that weekend represented my "rock bottom." I'd have to get comfortable with clichés, because much as I'd tried to think of myself as different or special, I would soon find out that all addicts are pretty much the same, and that I was one of them.

Frightened by what my life had become, and my sudden strong impulse to end it, I called a psychologist friend of mine, Dr. Frank Cummings, who had often testified for the prosecution as an expert witness in Calumet County criminal and juvenile cases. I didn't know where else to turn.

After speaking to me in his office, his small dog watching me intently while I spoke, helping to assess the new patient, Frank got on the phone to the intake staff at Gentle Path, an addiction treatment facility in Hattiesburg, Mississippi, a little city only known to me at the time as the college town of Green Bay Packers legend Brett Favre. Frank told me that "a famous golfer" had attended the sexual addiction treatment program there about a year earlier, and that Gentle Path's program, supervised by Dr. Patrick Carnes, was exactly what I needed. I wasn't so sure, but then, I was no longer sure of anything.

The next morning, Monday, I flew to New Orleans, the closest airport I could find to Hattiesburg. Alone in a Hattiesburg motel that evening, I felt lost. I texted a few of my friends and received no answers. I'd already become poison. To take the edge off, I popped an extra Xanax and an Ambien for sleep. I arrived at Gentle Path at 9 AM the next day, where several staff members met me in the lobby and introduced me to my primary therapist, a soft-spoken, middle-aged African American gentleman named Thomas.

At that time, Gentle Path was a collection of twenty-two patients, twenty male and two female, all suffering from what is clumsily called "sexual addiction." Sometimes referred to as "hypersexuality" or "sexual compulsivity," I was told it all means the same thing—the person "medicates" feelings and stressors in their lives with sex, in a compulsive and personally damaging manner. Lonely, or hungry, or angry, or tired? Sex. Things go wrong in your life, you have sex. Things go great, and it's time to celebrate—you use sex, just as other addicts might use chemicals. Sex is your drug of choice. Like any addictive behavior, you become powerless to control it, and your life becomes increasingly unmanageable.

My life had become about as unmanageable as I could envision. Five days before, I was getting along just fine, a well-respected district attorney, an accomplished and well-respected trial lawyer, father to a straight-A MBA student, living in a tastefully appointed condo in a town I loved, and happily dating a few wonderful women. Now I found myself sitting in the lobby of an inpatient sex addiction treatment facility in some 100-degree Mississippi town, having fled a media shit storm feeding on the familiar combination of sex and politics, chemical abuse, and the inevitable fall from grace. As the intake process continued, I broke down. Between the nurse's checkup and the explanation of meal and programming schedules, I began crying and couldn't stop. I was so tired, and so ashamed.

It was another five days before I moved past feeling I was in the wrong place, that I was not like "these guys." These guys, the other guys in my group, were sick. They had engaged in horrific behaviors, hurting those closest to them, abusing power and privilege, and feeling entitled to sexually act out wherever and whenever they chose. They were selfish, some diagnosed as clinically narcissistic. They were all things I was, but much worse—or so I thought.

"I don't belong here," I told the treatment director. "Discharge me."

"Why not give it three more days?" she said. "If you still want to go home then, we'll put you on a plane. But, in those three days, try to see in what ways you are like the other patients, and have common issues, not how you are different."

Grudgingly, I agreed.

In my individual and small-group therapy, Thomas pushed me to realize that there wasn't anything special about me or my problems. I was, Thomas said, a "blade of grass" in a whole field of addicts, all of us exactly the same. It doesn't matter if you used to be an attorney or a congressman, an elite athlete, a ditch digger, or a bum: you're an addict in treatment, trying to get better—that's it.

Thirteen hours a day of some form of therapy. Some flavor of twelve-step meetings every day. I learned that addicts stop using the executive decision-making part of their brains, the prefrontal cortex, and start using the midbrain, also aptly referred to as the pleasure center. The ability to weigh the consequences of your behaviors is all but removed; there is no considering the hurt you may cause others; no empathy—just the powerful impulse to do whatever is required to get your next hit of dopamine. When you ask an addict, "What were you thinking?" the straight answer is that they literally weren't.

You can't dispense with a lifetime of emotional issues, shame, and addictive behaviors in a six-week program. The best you can hope for is to interrupt the addiction cycle, and to discover and develop the tools you'll need to get better. Gentle Path gave me that.

After being excoriated in the press for having been too lenient in their treatment of my 2009 texting incident, the OLR decided to reopen and reconsider my case, filing (and publicly releasing) a formal ethics complaint against me at the end of November 2011. They also announced their intention to suspend my law license.

In the complaint, the OLR included other allegations—for instance, me sexting an Oklahoma City law student, and even a sexual assault, a charge the DOJ, which had concluded their own criminal and ethics investigation of me earlier in 2011, had already found "without merit."

After announcing them publicly, the OLR later quietly dismissed the other allegations. There was no press release announcing the dismissals. No live press conference. As far as the general public knew, I was a rapist and a serial sexter. The news coverage surrounding the ethics case was brutal, resurrecting the original texting scandal, and publicizing and bringing back shameful memories of my worst behaviors—the inappropriate comments I'd made to coworkers, the women I'd pursued on dating sites while still married.

I worked hard to rebuild my reputation, but the scandal followed me wherever I went thereafter, and once *Making a Murderer* was released, the hope of living down the sins of my past was extinguished once and for all.

———————

I am proud to say that, despite losing friends and my career as a prosecutor, despite being ruined financially and professionally, I have held fast to my recovery and the things I learned in treatment. For four years after release from the treatment center, I spent every Saturday morning "checking in" on conference calls with six to eight men from the program. We supported each other through the difficult journey of recovery, and they deserve my thanks for helping me get better, and stay better. The SAA, NA, and SLAA meetings I attended were also invaluable.

The Wisconsin Lawyers Assistance Program (WisLAP), and my attorney mentor, David Lasker, assigned to work with me weekly for two years, were critically important to my reintegration into the legal profession. Unfortunately, attorneys have one of the highest rates of addiction and depression of any profession. The competitive work atmosphere, a tendency toward high standards and perfectionism, and the risk of harsh consequences for professional misconduct all combine to create a systemic obstacle to lawyers seeking assistance.

I'm proud of how far I've come. Now a criminal defense attorney, I find it is a rare case in which drugs, alcohol, or other addictive dynamics didn't play at least some part in the client's misbehavior. I've never forgotten what it felt like to hit bottom, and helping others find a way to avoid that moment, or move on from it, also gives me hope, and a sense of purpose.

Oftentimes, I wonder where I'd be if I hadn't gotten help. And once in a while, I wonder whether things might have been different for Steven Avery if he'd been forced to confront his own narcissism and entitlement, if he'd found a way to manage his anger that didn't involve lashing out at others. I wonder, too, how things might have been different for Teresa Halbach.

CHAPTER THIRTEEN

The Vast, Fantastical Police Conspiracy

D o you believe in fairy tales? I hope so, because you're going to need a downright childlike ability to suspend disbelief in order to get your arms around all of the coincidences—the circumstances that would have had to line up smoothly and perfectly, the conclusions defying all logic—required for law enforcement to pin Teresa Halbach's murder on an innocent Steven Avery.

Let's lay out this spun-up conspiracy. Have some aspirin handy. It's going to make your head hurt.

Deputies Lenk and Colborn, with no history of misconduct or dishonesty, would have had to locate Teresa Halbach's RAV4, determine that Teresa had been murdered (or decide to kill her themselves), and drive the SUV from wherever it was found to hide it at Avery's Auto Salvage, without being detected, sometime

151

between October 31st and November 5th, 2005. They must have known that Teresa was last seen at the Avery property on the date of her disappearance, unless by an incredible stroke of luck the person they chose to "set up" for her murder just happened to be the last person to see her alive. Nobody can see them plant Teresa's license plates in a junked vehicle on the lot. No Avery can find Teresa's car before other, less crooked, cops do, or before it's stumbled upon by citizen searchers.

They would need Teresa's blood (to spread around the back of the SUV); they would need Avery's blood (not the vial of blood in the clerk's office, as that contained EDTA, but blood from the "actively bleeding" Avery himself); they would need the body of the twenty-five-year-old victim, which these officers must have been prepared to mutilate and burn. Her body couldn't have been burned and broken already when they found it, remember, or they'd have had no way to know for sure it was Teresa.

Later, they'd have to sneak onto the Avery property, coming within twenty feet of Steve's back door, to distribute her bones, a tooth, and a rivet from her jeans in the fire pit—remembering to burn some additional tires to intertwine fragile bone fragments into the steel belts, and using Steve's rake so that bits of the same belts could later be recovered from between its tines. For some reason, they must decide it would be best if the bones were found in more than one place, so they'd have to deposit four of the larger bones in the burn barrel behind the Dasseys' residence. Busy night for Andy and Jim!

It goes without saying that nobody could see the officers burning Teresa's body or chopping it up, or observe them planting the tiny and incredibly brittle pieces of bone in the Avery burn pit and the Dassey burn barrel—and this "nobody" includes Steve's loud and protective dog, Bear. They'd also have to hope that several citizens saw Avery with a large bonfire, at the exact location they chose for their bone planting and on the very evening that Teresa went missing. Andy and Jim would be busy *and* lucky—spectacularly so!

But we're just getting started.

These ruthlessly corrupt cops would have to slip into Calumet County evidence lockup or the Madison crime lab, depending on the date, and "borrow" Steven Avery's rifle (the same gun that deposited eleven shell casings found in his garage during the original search). Here's where it gets a little more difficult . . . they had to shoot the rifle, collect the bullet fragment, return to their secret stash of Teresa's DNA, and plant her DNA on the bullet fragment, and then plant that bullet in the Avery garage, under an air compressor, sometime before March 1st, 2006. They couldn't leave footprints in the snow that led to the garage, and they had to hope that someone would tell the police that the murder happened in the garage, so that law enforcement would get a search warrant to look for the bullet.

If you've managed to follow along so far, it gets even more complicated. These two dirty, dastardly cops had to collect non-blood DNA from Steven Avery (not an easy task, as any perspiration they collected had to have Avery's skin cells sloughed in it) and plant that DNA on Teresa's car key (with the blue fob that matched the National Guard lanyard in her locked SUV), and plant the key in Avery's bedroom, while under observation by Calumet evidence techs. They also had to plant some of this non-blood DNA under the hood of the victim's SUV, on the hood latch, either before it was discovered or while it was held in the custody of either the Madison crime lab or the Calumet County Sheriff's Department. Then they had to hope that Steven's nephew (or another person willing to implicate himself) would "someday" tell officers that Avery reached under the SUV hood, the tip needed to corroborate the hood latch story, leading to that DNA's collection in April of 2006.

OK, almost done. Andy and Jim had to obtain the victim's phone, digital camera, and PDA. They had to burn those items, in *Avery's* burn barrel (the same barrel that Blaine Dassey and Robert Fabian saw Avery himself burning items in on October 31st—another stroke of luck for Andy and Jim!), sometime before November 5th, without anyone noticing, which would take hours. They lucked out again when Brendan Dassey told investigators that Uncle Steve burned the contents of Teresa's purse in his own burn barrel.

If the cops weren't the ones to kill Teresa themselves, they'd have to be lucky enough that whatever method chosen by the "real killer" left no inconsistencies between the bullets they planted, the two skull fragments with gunshot holes surrounded by tiny lead particles, and the findings of the forensic anthropologist and forensic pathologist. They couldn't leave any prints or DNA themselves, naturally, and neither could the "real killer," or, if he or she did, his or her prints and DNA couldn't be in the DOJ identification system. And finally, no witness, or potential member of the conspiracy, could talk about it anytime thereafter—ever.

Oh, and by the way, nobody else *anywhere* could see Teresa alive after she was at the salvage property on October 31st, as that alone would totally destroy the "Avery did it" charade. She couldn't use her phone after she arrived at the Avery property—ever. Steven Avery couldn't have an alibi. Luckily, he and Teresa had the same two-hour period of cell phone inactivity after her visit, before her cell phone was disabled permanently; luckily he'd chosen to take off work the afternoon of October 31st for the first time ever. Luckily, he specifically requested Teresa as a photographer, and made some blocked calls to her that day, and then a non-blocked call after she left, and lied in early interviews about whether Teresa showed up at all, and about whether he had a fire that night, all of which helped him look suspicious. Avery was a real help to his own framing—Andy and Jim owe him big-time.

You have to assume that these guys hated Avery enough that they were willing to risk not only losing their jobs, but also going to prison themselves for the murder of Teresa Halbach and/or for planting evidence. That's a bushel of hate. But neither Lenk nor Colborn faced financial pain from Avery's lawsuit against Manitowoc County. In fact—pop that last aspirin, and maybe pour yourself a drink too—Andy and Jim both thought Steven Avery should win his case. Two veteran cops, who had heard

"I'm innocent, Officer," more times than they could remember, believed a local man deserved a payday at the expense of the sheriff's department.

"I thought Steven, whose kids went to school with my kids, and whose tow trucks the department used from time to time, deserved to get paid," Colborn said. "I kind of felt bad for the guy."

That's sympathy, friends, not thrumming animus.

Jim Lenk remembers the day Teresa's RAV4 was found. "As soon as I rolled up on the salvage yard, that very first day, I knew we would be under a microscope, scrutinized and watched every step of the way. Nobody could have planted evidence at that scene even if they wanted to. The allegations—planting evidence, and that we conspired to get Avery convicted—are just ridiculous, almost fantastical."

Incredibly, many of the forty million *Making a Murderer* viewers believed that fantastical story rather than accept the obvious answer—that Avery did it. To one degree or another, the reputations of many devoted members of law enforcement were damaged in order that the defense, and *Making a Murderer*, could present this convoluted theory—for which there was no proof—as a possibility.

"Game on!" said defense attorney Jerry Buting into the camera, co-cheerleader-in-chief for the story of a vast and fantastical police conspiracy. But it wasn't a game, of course. And the truth about what happened to Teresa Halbach isn't so complicated. It's a simple, sad story—nothing like a fairy tale at all.

CHAPTER FOURTEEN

The Aftermath

I won't tell you where in Wisconsin I live now. I've escaped the torches and pitchforks that descended upon me in Superior, the small port city where I lived when *Making a Murderer* was released. I'm happy here, in this new place.

I'm semiretired. I declared bankruptcy in 2012, and draw a state pension from twenty-five years in the prosecution business. I'm a rabid Packers fan—required in Wisconsin. I play guitar, and am hoping to get a band back together. My girlfriend and I head out for a typical Midwestern fish fry most Friday nights, and stroll through the farmer's market on Saturday mornings. I spend more time with my son, Andy, who relocated nearby and now manages two restaurants.

Life is slow, but intentionally so these days. I subscribe to Netflix.

All told, I received more than 4,000 death threats and hate-filled messages—some brutally specific—after *Making a Murderer* debuted:

I watched the Netflix show—you were a total disgrace. You should be disbarred and imprisoned for a lot longer than Steven Avery and Brendan Dassey's combined sentences. Your obsession with winning the case with no regard for the truth left the real killer out there—nice going.

I hope your wife and children—if any—dumped your sorry, fat, licentious ass. I can't imagine their shame and embarrassment at being related to you let alone continuing any kind of relationship with you. If I were a kid of yours, I would move as far from you as I could, change my name, and tell anyone who asked that my dad died way, way back.

Have you ever done a single kind or charitable thing in your entire worthless life? You really are one of the lowest and most disgusting creatures that has ever crawled the earth.

You wrongfully convicted an innocent man, you knew this, and that makes you guilty, in a court of the public, you should be held accountable, I wish they still hung people or stoned them to death just for you.

I just got off my knees praying to God to inflict more pain and suffering in your life than anything mentioned in the Old Testament. No punishment or suffering you could endure could be enough. I pray you watch your wife and children die a painful gruesome death in front of your eyes. I pray you suffer in ways I don't even have words to describe.

A few times, the social media flogging turned into something else; a couple of Avery supporters came to Wisconsin to harass me in person. When a man named Daniel Luke traveled all the way from Oregon in January 2016 to stake out my office—and film our confrontation for YouTube—the cops had to threaten an arrest to get him to leave. He later returned to my office parking lot to leave "some DNA" on my door handles, and film my license plate for the benefit of future vandals.

Before the harassment slowed in 2016, I had replaced a broken rear window, a cracked driver's window (shot with a pellet gun), two broken windshield wipers, and couldn't leave the house without wondering whether today was the day someone would "even the score" for the nation's newest hero, Steven Avery. Given the number of people who promised to, I didn't think I was overreacting. Neither did the local police.

I've struggled to let go of my anger, tried to accept that I can't control the opinions and actions of others. My past doesn't define who I am today, and I won't allow armchair experts, trained at the Netflix School of Law, to define me either. But I won't deny that it's hard to see conspiracy theories embraced over facts, to see what

I've always regarded as one of my greatest accomplishments—the successful prosecution of Steven Avery—characterized as incompetence or prosecutorial misconduct. A man from California wrote to suggest history would recount my story alongside that of a fellow named Adolf Hitler. I was compared to Ted Bundy, Hannibal Lecter, and The Grinch Who Stole Christmas in an internet "Worst Villains in History—Real or Fictional" play-off bracket. Worst villain in *history*? For doing my job? For convincing twelve citizens from Manitowoc that the evidence was overwhelming, pointed to one obvious suspect, and argued that this man should be held accountable for the death of the twenty-five-year-old photographer whose body was found almost literally at his doorstep?

I have specific goals for this book. In outlining the case against Steven Avery more completely than has been done before, I hope this book flips the public narrative of the Avery case back to before December 18th, 2015, when cops and prosecutors in the case were still generally considered the "good guys," and Avery was accurately viewed as a ruthless convicted killer. I hope seeing what *wasn't* shown in *Making a Murderer*—the facts omitted, the testimony spliced and truncated—encourages viewers to turn a more critical eye on the media they consume. I realize this outcome is unlikely, given the four Emmy awards taken home by the filmmakers and the breathless media coverage of *Making a Murderer*'s upcoming second season, but a guy can hope.

I also hope this book will shed some light on *why* Avery killed Teresa, a question that, to this day, over eleven years after the murder, remains unanswered.

Many media pundits and Netflix subscribers claim that it doesn't make sense for Avery, poised to settle his multimillion-dollar federal lawsuit, to jeopardize his relatively bright future by killing a young woman. Time after time, over the years, I returned to the question myself: Why did Steven Avery rape and kill Teresa Halbach? Because they don't think like Avery—thankfully—ordinary, logical citizens have trouble conceiving of the answer. The trial didn't answer the question, nor was it intended to. Most people probably assume he acted on impulse, that killing Teresa was an uncontrollable heat-of-the-moment act, or even a sexually charged crime of passion.

But Avery is obsessive. In jailhouse phone calls, he'd get stuck on a topic, especially if somebody had been critical of him. Steven feels every slight to the core and never lets anything go. It eats at him, week after week, month after month, and year after year.

In prison for the assault of Penny Beernsten, Steven sat in his six-by-eight cell, day after day, focused on what he intended to do upon his release: abduct, rape, torture, and kill a young woman. Avery said as much to fellow inmate Jessey W. Werlien, and even showed Werlien drawings of the "torture chamber" he intended to construct—his prison sidekick assisted with the artwork. Teresa's future abduction, rape, and death were recounted at the Green Bay Correctional Institution to any inmate who would listen. Avery had planned the brutal attack down to the location (the Avery salvage yard) and the best manner of disposing of the body (to burn it). Heat, especially a big fire, is the one thing that destroys all DNA left on or in the body, semen included. Eliminating DNA at the crime scene, Steve knew, was the best way to avoid having a murder pinned on him. He'd become somewhat of a DNA expert during his eighteen years of incarceration, benefitting from his front-row seat to scientific advances in the field.

Steven didn't have a specific woman in mind, of course. Teresa Halbach just happened to fit the template of his fantasy. This fantasy woman wasn't meant to stand in place of Penny Beernsten; she was a proxy for every woman Avery had ever felt wronged by. This murder was what he felt he was "owed" for the eighteen years the State of Wisconsin took from him.

The question isn't really why Steve killed Teresa, it's when. I believe that in his mind, he killed Teresa Halbach the day he went to prison for a sexual assault he didn't commit, and he killed her every day for the next eighteen years. When he lured her to his trailer on October 31st, 2005, it was neither a crime of impulse nor of logical calculation. There was no thought to potential consequences. Teresa's death was by then a foregone conclusion.

———————————

Avery has given at least nine different stories of his contact with Teresa on that day, not counting conflicting versions he's given to reporters. Innocent people don't lie about basic, central questions in a murder investigation, like whether they had contact with the victim the day she was killed. Consider the following, and try to think of an innocent reason for his inconsistent accounts:

10/31 (approx. 4:30 PM): Steven tells Chuck Avery and Robert Fabian that Teresa never showed up that day.

10/31 (approx. 8:57 PM): Steven makes no mention of Teresa Halbach's visit in his recorded call with Jodi Stachowski.

11/3 (afternoon): Steven tells Scott Bloedorn, Teresa's roommate, that Teresa "never showed up" for her appointment on October 31st, and is upset that he was even contacted in connection with the disappearance.

11/3 (between 4:30 and 5 PM): Steven calls to tell *Auto Trader* employees that Teresa never showed up on October 31st, but that she called to tell him she couldn't make it. He asked that they reschedule the appointment.

*Note: Steven speaks to his nephew Bobby Dassey sometime after the November 3rd *Auto Trader* call, and for the first time realizes that there is a witness to Teresa Halbach's presence on the property that Halloween afternoon— Bobby himself.

11/3 (between 6:30 and 7:30 PM): Steven finally concedes to Sergeant Andy Colborn that Teresa *did* show up Monday afternoon, saying he saw her through the window, but never made face-to-face contact with her.

11/4 (approx. 10:20 PM): Steven tells Detective Remiker and Lieutenant Lenk that Teresa showed up, he did meet with her, and in fact she was in his residence, where he paid her for the photo shoot Monday afternoon.

11/4 (unknown time): Steven tells David Beach that Teresa showed up about 2 PM and that he showed her a couple of vehicles and she took pictures.

11/5 (11:30 AM): Steven tells Marinette County detective Anthony O'Neill that Teresa showed up between 2 and 2:30, he saw her take photos of the van, he went to meet and pay her *outside*, and they exchanged small talk for about five minutes.

11/6 (8 AM): Steven tells Marinette County detective Anthony O'Neill and DCI agent Kim Skorlinski that Teresa showed up, and Steven went out to meet her. He paid her and gave her a note with the price he was asking. Teresa gave him an *Auto Trader* book, but never left the car.

———————————

Beginning six years after the trial, in January 2013, Steven Avery and I exchanged a series of letters. He knew that I was no longer a DA and no longer represented the state, and he invited me to visit him at the prison in Boscobel, Wisconsin. He said he had questions for me, and implored me to be "totally honest" with him. I was hopeful that this signaled Avery's willingness to, at last, be candid about Teresa's death, now that he'd lost his appeals.

I arranged to meet Avery on February 8th, 2013, but he failed to include me on his visitors' list. By the time this oversight was resolved, the Wisconsin Department of Corrections hierarchy decided they were less than thrilled with the idea of a Kratz-Avery reunion. The Boscobel warden rejected Avery's request for our sit-down interview, citing the possibility that the visit might "hinder the inmate's reintegration into the community" (a strange reason, given Avery is serving a sentence that means he will *never* be reintegrated into the community).

A few months later, in another bizarre letter, Avery requested that I handle his appeal. Needless to say, I declined.

On August 28th, 2015, less than four months before *Making a Murderer* was released, Steven Avery reached out to me for the final time, asking that I investigate possible fingerprint evidence from several new "suspects"—including members of his immediate family and a family friend—who might have been responsible for setting him up.

Then, I knew that Steven Avery would never reveal what occurred on October 31st, 2005; he had no interest in coming clean. He would never say he did it. He would never say he was sorry. He'd keep trying to manipulate anyone and everyone who came into contact with him, anyone who might offer him a

6-18-2013

Hi Mr. Kratz

You dont work for the State no more So why dont you take my appeal! You now the Case and you got Candy Avery. See we can all get Money together this would be the truth that She Candy did it good!

See you can Call up here a talk to me as a Attorney on my Case!!! action right?

Thank you,

Steven Avery

You and a nother Attorney Can take it right?

let me know.

Soon

Letter from Steven, 6/18/2013

glimmer of hope for his freedom. I wrote and told him I was done with our correspondence.

―――――――――――

I'm often asked how my community perceives me now, more than a year after *Making a Murderer* characterized me as a deceitful and unethical bum. The thing about folks from Wisconsin is that, generally, everyone is pretty nice. I still get my share of stares, but most people are polite, many even supportive, or at least sensitive enough to recognize the difficult times I've been through.

The other dynamic at play, especially in northeastern Wisconsin (Manitowoc, Appleton, Green Bay), is that these are people who lived through the Avery trial in "real time"—and had the benefit of seeing the evidence as it actually unfolded and was presented in court—and they generally remain convinced of Steven Avery's guilt. *Making a Murderer* was still eight and a half years away when I convicted Steven in the spring of 2007, and no new evidence has emerged to reverse their opinions. Avery's new attorney, Kathleen Zellner, promised to identify the "real killer" within thirty days of accepting the post-conviction case in January 2016—this book is being completed in the fall of 2016, and I'm still waiting to hear who the mystery culprit was.

Candidly, it's not my work on the Avery case or even the aftermath of *Making a Murderer* that continues to stain my reputation in Wisconsin, but the 2010 texting scandal. I'm remembered not as the former Calumet County district attorney, or even as the Avery special prosecutor, but as the public official who sent sexually suggestive text messages to a bruised and battered crime victim. That—not the prosecution of Steven Avery—is what has prevented me from living a life free of shame and regret. The sexting story is what led my dentist to suggest that I seek dental treatments elsewhere. It led the Wisconsin attorney malpractice insurance company to deny me coverage, because "our members won't want to be affiliated with someone like you." Most of my former friends and colleagues from before the scandal never contact me—they don't invite me to get-togethers, or training conferences, or send well-wishes via email or social media. I remain a pariah in most professional circles, and likely will indefinitely. Make no mistake, I'm *not* a victim in this situation, except of my own poor decision making, and I don't blame others for excluding me now.

What I lost in the scandal pales, believe it or not, in comparison with what I gained when I learned to control the destructive temptations of my addictive personality. I have my self-respect back; I enjoy the peace that comes with no longer needing to worry about who I've lied to, or cheated on, or screwed over recently. I don't use prescription drugs, nor feel the urge to anymore. I continue to reach out to my sex addiction treatment alums, as needed, to ensure that my addictive personality remains dormant. I like who I've become and am proud to have faced my personal and professional crises head-on. I'm not making excuses.

There may need to be future discussion of Brendan Dassey's saga, given the number of unresolved issues surrounding his case, many raised in the federal district court decision. These include the impact of deficient representation on the outcome of his trial; his claims of having given a "false confession" to police (it would be nice to someday reconcile the many versions he provided); the impact his family had on his plea decisions; the impact counsel for a convicted codefendant (Dean Strang) had when recommending to Brendan's mother that he should proceed to trial rather than take a plea, as "his case has gotten stronger as a result of the Avery conviction"; and finally whether another person or persons may have assisted in the crimes committed that Halloween on the Avery salvage property.

But as for Steven Alan Avery? He's right where he belongs, in a maximum-security prison, doing what convicted murderers who've enjoyed the spotlight do: cycling through female admirers of all ages, considering a jailhouse marriage, hoping the next wave of publicity washes him back onto the streets of his hometown. I don't think it will. I think Steven Avery's quarter-hour of true crime fame, a period that energized and empowered internet detectives and created improbable social activists across socioeconomic lines—at the expense of attention to his victim—will end. A notoriety fueled by lucky timing and an insatiable, unaccountable digital media will fade.

And so, for now, as Steven Avery himself would say when concluding his jailhouse calls, there's "nuttin' else" to talk about.

ACKNOWLEDGMENTS

The investigation and trial of Steven Avery and Brendan Dassey occupied eighteen months of the time of the Calumet County Sheriff's Department and District Attorney Office—time taken away from the citizens of Calumet County, Wisconsin. Although it was my honor and privilege to advocate for the rights of the Halbach family, it was a Manitowoc County case, and my accepting appointment as Special Prosecutor required the allocation of our county resources.

I therefore offer my sincere thanks to the men and women of Calumet County Law Enforcement for the professionalism and competence showed during this prosecution effort, and the resiliency exhibited in absorbing the aftermath. Special thanks goes to then Calumet County Sheriff Jerry Pagel for his leadership and support, and Mark Wiegert for his tenacity and grit as lead investigator. Calumet County was fortunate to have such fine law enforcement representation.

Thanks to the Calumet County DA's Office support staff who not only dedicated countless extra hours assisting with the Halbach case, but who ensured the smooth operation of the office, oftentimes in my absence. Shirley Gregory, Michelle Moehn, Amanda Bunnell, Lea Calaway, Llonda Thomas, and Julie Leverenz will always occupy a warm and special place in my heart for their fierce loyalty, and especially for putting up with my idiosyncrasies.

Special thanks to my Assistant DA, Jeff Froehlich, who not only assisted with the Halbach prosecution, but who covered the entire Calumet County case load when I was immersed in the Avery and Dassey prosecutions. Jeff was also required to step in and provide professional stability after my resignation and personal collapse in 2010, and has thereafter continued to dispense justice as Calumet County Circuit Judge.

Having chosen to say nothing since the Avery trial started, I witnessed firsthand how the allegations of corruption and dishonesty silently impacted two well-respected law enforcement professionals for many years. Jim Lenk and Andy Colborn have endured professional and personal attacks for over ten years (and counting), having been identified as the two officers who "framed" Steven Avery for the murder of Teresa Halbach. My heartfelt thanks to both for choosing to participate in this book, to set the record straight, and remind the world that our reputations, forged over our lifetime, should never be the subject of defense counsel or media-fueled blood sport.

Tom Fassbender provided insight and perspective, not just in the Avery investigation, but in helping me write this book. For his professional expertise, and for his unwavering personal support, I thank you, my friend. Special thanks also to Brenda Schuler who provided hours of research and fact-checking for this project, and who has since become an amazing friend and confidante.

Life has provided challenges since November 2005. No set of family and friends should be required to withstand the insensitivity and indifference as has been exhibited toward those loved ones surviving Teresa Halbach. From the investigation, through the trial, sentencing, appeals, and media circus, the friends and family of Teresa have exhibited class and restraint—I pray the loving memory of Teresa continues to sustain you through your lives until you can someday be reunited.

As it turns out, those members of "Team Kratz" haven't exactly had an easy ride since 2005 themselves, and my shameful personal behaviors have made loving and supporting me anything but popular. But for my family who has stuck with me, and the handful of friends who haven't cared what others may have thought, I owe you my everlasting gratitude for choosing to stand at my side.

And finally, to my son, Andrew, who not only has been the one constant throughout my life, but who put his career on hold to help his dad research and write a book, I am incredibly proud of you, and love you with all my heart.

DATE			